On Board with the Duke

On Board with the Duke

John Wayne and the Wild Goose

Captain Bert Minshall
with Clark Sharon

SEVEN LOCKS PRESS

To my brother Ken Minshall, who made it all possible.

Library of Congress Cataloging-in-Publication Data

Minshall, Bert.
    On Board with the Duke: John Wayne and the Wild Goose/
by Bert Minshall with Clark Sharon.
        p.   cm.
ISBN 0-929765-13-3: $39.95
        1. Wayne, John, 1907–1979. 2. Wild Goose (Yacht). 3. Motion picture
actors and actresses—United States—Biography. I. Sharon, Clark. II. Title.
PN2287.W454M56 1992
791.43'028'092—dc20
[B]   92-27938
                                      CIP

Published in 1992 by Seven Locks Press, Washington, D. C.

Edited and designed by Amy Janello and Brennon Jones
Produced by Jones & Janello, New York

Printed by Southeastern Printing in the United States of America

Front jacket photo by Bert Minshall
Back jacket photo by Archive Photos
Photos on pages 2–3, 7 by Phil Stern
Photo on page 6 by Bert Minshall

CONTENTS

PREFACE

John Wayne was my boss and friend for the last sixteen years of his life. I started those years, fresh from Liverpool, as a deckhand aboard his 136-foot converted U.S. Navy minesweeper, the *Wild Goose*. I ended them as the ship's last skipper under Duke's ownership.

The great, aging yacht was the actor's proudest possession as well as a much cherished floating retreat and playground. She was the sort of ship you'd expect John Wayne to own . . . big, rugged, comfortable, impressive. Few stars would have had the money or grit to take on such a formidable pain in the pocketbook. But to Duke, owning the *Wild Goose* capped a life that had been lived to the hilt. She was more than status symbol . . . she was an extension of himself.

I helped raise Duke's children Aissa, Ethan and Marisa aboard that wonderful old boat. Duke took me into his life and his family's life. I was lucky, and I knew it.

Duke's life and times aboard the *Wild Goose*, all the places he sailed in her, all the humor and drama and pleasures that took place on her decks, are known to only a handful of friends and crew members. It is a largely unreported part of Duke's life that I've felt for a long time should be told before there's no one left to do so.

I guess you could say this book is a combination adventure yarn and love story. The love, I unabashedly admit, is for Duke, his family and the shipmates who shared my good fortune over the years—and for the magnificent ship that made it all possible.

I miss Duke and my life aboard the *Wild Goose*. This book, and the pictures in it, are a way for me to hold onto both, to keep them always with me. That is why this book is as much my personal diary as it is a record for those who want to know what it was like to sail with a man who has moved squarely into legend. It's my life, and through the telling, a great part of Duke's as well.

JOHN WAYNE MAKES HIS POINT
CLEAR TO BERT MINSHALL. AL
SATTERWHITE/IMAGE BANK

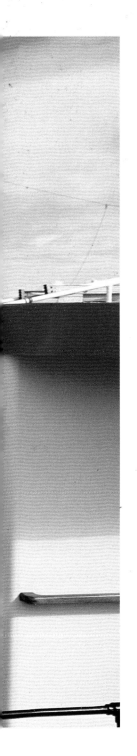

PROLOGUE

John Wayne, standing on the upper deck of the *Wild Goose*, smeared head to toe with suntan lotion, was angry as hell.

"I'M GONNA SHOOT FOUR PEOPLE IF MARISA GETS HURT ON THAT THING!" he roared as a skiboat towing a small plywood sled sliced across the yacht's stern. Clinging to the bucking platform, laughing and having the time of her life, was the actor's eight-year-old daughter, Marisa Carmela Wayne. Instantly, the smile left the girl's face as her father's words boomed over the water.

As driver of the skiboat, I was one of the four people Duke had in his cross hairs. The others were his two older children, Aissa and Ethan, riding with me and a teenage friend of Aissa's who had joined little Marisa on the sled. Duke obviously thought we were going too fast for his youngest daughter's safety. I didn't think Marisa was in any danger, but I wasn't about to risk another outburst. I backed down on the throttle. It was a very disappointed Marisa whom I towed slowly back to the big yacht.

The *Wild Goose* had been anchored for several days now in this calm bay located about a dozen miles from Acapulco. She was a beautiful vessel, her white hull rising clean and bright from the deep blue water. A tricolor Mexican courtesy flag snapped gently from the mast behind the wheel-house. An idyllic scene. Except for the sight of my angry boss waiting for us on the enclosed afterdeck.

Duke met me at the stern gunwale after I'd tied off the skiboat. He didn't say anything. Only glared. With all that lotion on, he looked not only very angry, but very slippery. Then he strode off. No chewing out, but as the responsible adult of the bunch, I knew I was in his personal doghouse.

I did my best to avoid him the rest of the day. He didn't say two words to me the entire afternoon and evening. Although I felt he'd been overprotective of Marisa's safety, I hated the thought that somehow I'd disappointed him. As the *Goose*'s first mate, as well as shipboard guardian and companion to his children, his trust in me was complete. I turned in that night to dream troubled dreams.

The next morning I went about my chores, which included helping the ship's two deckhands swab down the dew-wetted decks. I was mopping outside the master stateroom when the cabin door opened and out stepped Duke. First thing in the morning he liked to walk twenty or so brisk laps around the upper deck. He spotted me as he shut the door.

"Good morning, Bert."

"Good morning, Mr. Wayne."

Even after ten years aboard the *Goose*, I still didn't feel comfortable addressing him by his famous nickname. At least not while on duty. Off the boat, however, he insisted I call him Duke. I sank the mop in the bucket and stepped back to let him pass.

"You about done?" he asked as he zipped his windbreaker and adjusted his golf cap.

"I can finish later."

Perhaps he sensed that the previous afternoon was still very much on my mind. He put his hands on his hips and lowered his head a moment, as if in thought, then looked up.

"Listen, Bert," he said, standing close to me, "before you go, I want to apologize for losing my temper with you yesterday."

He'd caught me off guard. I hadn't expected an apology.

"Oh, that's okay, Mr. Wayne. Don't worry about it."

"Well, I *do* worry about it because I like you very much."

I was at a loss for words. Not waiting for a reply, he marched off on his first circuit of the deck, leaving me holding a bucket of dirty water.

I made my way down to the maindeck. As I stowed the mop and bucket in a bulkhead locker, I heard the soft thud of Duke's rubber-soled deckshoes directly above me. I looked up and listened to his retreating footsteps. At that moment I would gladly have eaten hot lead for him at ten cents a pound.

Good Luck

What I knew about John Wayne in October of 1963 you could've fit into an English teacup. I was thirty years old, working as a ship's carpenter in and around Liverpool, the great seaport on England's northwest coast. Every weekday morning I made the short ferry ride across the Mersey from my home in Wallasey, a pleasant middle-class suburb where I had grown up with my five brothers. I wasn't much of a movie fan in those days. I don't think I ever saw a John Wayne flick. Not that I probably didn't *sit* through a few. The darkened balcony of the Capital Theater in my hometown wasn't where the local mates went for serious film watching. It was where we took our girls for an afternoon of mutual groping.

Yet even the charms of the Capital Theater balcony couldn't lessen the dread I felt heading into another long English winter, when the fierce chill winds would come blowing in from off the Irish Sea. I was working in a dead-end job with no real hope of escape. I was going nowhere . . . except back and forth across the cold Mersey on a ferryboat.

I have brotherly nepotism to thank for the change in my life that led me to John Wayne and the *Wild Goose*. My older brother Ken was engineer aboard the *Goose*, which had recently crossed the Atlantic from America and was temporarily moored at Barcelona, Spain. On a rare visit home he casually asked if I'd like to help crew the ship on her return voyage to the States. The yacht was short a deckhand. I didn't hesitate to accept.

At the time, the chance to meet and work for Duke Wayne—as he was known to millions of fans—didn't excite me as much as the adventure of an ocean crossing. Then there was the golden lure of the *Goose's* final destination and new home port—Newport Beach, California. Say the word California to any of my mates in Wallasey and immediately images of palm trees and beautiful girls would come to mind.

But for me, California was another word for sunshine. A few years earlier I'd served a stint with the Royal Air Force (jockeying trucks, however, not Spitfires). I'd spent most of my two-year hitch stationed in the perpetual sunshine of Aden, then a British colony on the southern coast of the Arabian peninsula. I quickly learned why only mad dogs and Englishmen go out in the midday sun. They see so bloody little of it back in England. I was soon hooked on the stuff. At last, I thought, here was my chance to get back to cloudless skies and warm, sunny days.

I spent a week wrapping up my affairs in England, then it was off by jetliner to Barcelona. When I first saw the *Wild Goose* moored to a concrete quay in the city's busy harbor I underwent nautical culture shock. What a far cry she was from the weather-beaten rust buckets that haunted the gray wharves of Liverpool and Berkenhead. The *Goose* looked like a floating Taj Mahal. Her white hull and bulkheads gleamed in the

THE *WILD GOOSE* IN THE HARBOR OF MONTE CARLO AFTER HER 1963 ATLANTIC CROSSING. CHIEF ENGINEER KEN MINSHALL CROSSES THE BOATDECK. *BLACK STAR PHOTO*

Spanish sunlight, decks scrubbed, brass polished. And for a private yacht, she was tremendous—at 136 feet nearly half the length of a soccer field. Her wheelhouse rose a good three stories above the waterline, while the foredeck looked big enough to hold a boxing ring. I climbed the yacht's boarding ladder onto the sidedeck, my worldly possessions crammed into one battered suitcase. Ken snapped my picture as I stood by the gunwale, a big grin on my face, wearing a new suit that was too big for me.

I didn't realize it at the time, but I was home.

BERT MINSHALL BOARDS THE *WILD GOOSE* FOR THE FIRST TIME, AT BARCELONA, SPAIN. *BERT MINSHALL PHOTO*

•

HOME IT MAY HAVE BEEN, BUT IT WOULD BE FIVE MONTHS AND SEVEN THOUSAND MILES before I finally met John Wayne.

Duke had left the ship shortly before my arrival to finish work on a film called *Circus World*, directed by his good friend Howard Hawks. Not until the following spring, after he had finished filming and attended to business matters back in Los Angeles, did he manage to rejoin the *Goose* at a small Mexican fishing village called La Paz near the Baja California tip.

Up to this point life aboard ship had resembled a working vacation. We'd spent long weeks in the sunny Caribbean, passed through the Panama Canal and spent still more weeks leisurely cruising up the Central American and Mexican coasts. We took our time, giving Duke a chance to catch up with us for the final leg of the yacht's journey to Newport Beach.

Duke arrived in La Paz via small plane. Accompanying him were his wife, Pilar, and their two young children, Aissa, eight, and Ethan, two. The actor also brought with him his valet, Fausto, and the valet's teenage son, Efrem—an extravagance that impressed me at the time. I never actually saw their arrival aboard ship, however. As they were climbing the boarding ladder from the yacht's tender, I was below deck attending to some last-minute chores. They ducked into their quarters on the maindeck before I could get even so much as a peek at my famous boss. It was a disappointment that would be remedied the following morning—and in memorable fashion.

Duke was drinking coffee in the main salon when the *Goose*'s skipper, Pete Stein, ushered me in for my official audience. I admit I was nervous as the legendary John Wayne stuck out a huge hand in my direction. Suddenly I regretted not having paid more attention to what was happening up on the screen at the Capital Theater. Even dressed in a wrinkled, loose-fitting shirt and baggy slacks, the man's physical impact was enormous. Over the years and long after our friendship was established, I never ceased to be a little bowled over by Duke's presence. He fairly oozed charisma.

My hand disappeared in his massive paw. His fingers were as big as two of mine. It was a hard, strong grip, but not crushing. Some of my nervousness gave way as the actor's friendly manner began to put me at ease. One of the things about Duke that relaxed me was, odd as it may seem, his obvious lack of hair. He didn't have much more than Ken, who sported only a light fringe on the sides. I thought it was surprisingly human of John Wayne to be bald.

Pete Stein, looking bored beyond comprehension, leaned against a bulkhead as Duke asked me a few questions about my home back in England (former home, as it would turn out), and we talked a little about the *Goose*. I don't remember much of what was said. Too excited to be paying close attention, I suppose. But I'll never forget what happened as that first brief meeting came to a close.

That morning I'd slipped on a brand new pair of expensive deckshoes. Now, I realized that Duke was staring at my feet. No doubt, I proudly thought, the sharp-looking footwear had caught his attention.

"New shoes, huh?" he asked, cocking his head a little.

Before I could answer, he cleared his throat with a sound that could have passed for that of a moose with bronchitis, and proceeded to spit with admirable accuracy all over my neatly tied laces. I jumped back, stunned. Pete suddenly appeared interested in what was going on. I looked down at my feet, not quite comprehending that John Wayne, the world's biggest movie star, had just spit on me.

Duke, looking serious, moved a step closer, put one of those huge hands on my shoulder, and imparted some timely advice.

"Always spit on new shoes, Bert," he drawled. "It's good luck."

DUKE WITH FAMILY IN MID-1960S (FROM LEFT), ETHAN, AISSA AND PILAR. *GLOBE PHOTOS*

First Days

With Duke finally aboard it was as if someone had switched on an electric current through the *Goose*'s seven-member crew. We no longer looked or acted like a bunch of laid-back pirates as we had the previous five months. Gone were the torn T-shirts and paint-splattered shorts. Clean and pressed tan uniforms were the order of the day. Chores were attended to on a much stricter schedule. We were finally fulfilling our purpose . . . to make shipboard life for Duke and his family as pleasant and hitch-free as possible.

I was as happy as I'd ever been in my life. Not only was it exciting having a movie star aboard, but there was a real camaraderie among the *Goose*'s crew. During our long voyage to La Paz I'd gotten to know my shipmates well, especially skipper Pete Stein.

Tough, sea-wise Pete Stein. An excellent navigator, a great storyteller, and a tremendous fan of J&B scotch. He liked to lace his shipboard coffee with scotch—a habit that sometimes led to near disaster, such as the time we stopped over at Gibraltar before our Atlantic crossing and he left the gearshifts engaged, sending the *Goose* into a concrete quay. Fortunately, that produced only an ugly gash in the yacht's bow that we repaired once we made Grenada in the Caribbean. We kidded Pete unmercifully about running the boat into the Rock of Gibraltar, but he took it good-naturedly. Over the years Duke always displayed a tolerant attitude toward Pete's drinking. Once, in response to a disparaging remark about the skipper's liquor lust, he responded, "I don't trust a man who doesn't drink." The rest of us in the crew figured he must have trusted Pete like no other man alive.

My best pal among the crew, and fellow deckhand, was Daly Davies, a cheerful New Zealand lad who delighted in scrambling the crew's sensibilities by setting off the ship's old general quarters siren in the dead of night. After a summer of bumming around Europe, Daly had joined the *Goose* in Barcelona a few weeks before me. Working aboard the yacht meant adventure and free passage back to the States, where he planned to attend college. Daly was the sparkplug among the crew, always ready for a joke or a good time. I had come to enjoy his boisterous company, although you had to watch him—he'd give a hot-foot to an angel for a laugh.

Rounding out the crew were Eduardo, a one-time lieutenant in the Mexican Navy and the *Goose*'s first mate; Tim, the capable assistant engineer from Newport Beach; Nina, Captain Pete's wife and seacook for this voyage; quiet Raul, the diminutive steward; and, of course, my brother Ken, who seemed to live in the engine room, loved the sea, and was so prone to motion sickness that a moderate swell forced him to stand watch with a bucket at the ready between his feet. Just in case.

The same morning Duke christened my new deck-shoes, Pete Stein introduced me to the actor's wife. Pilar was Duke's third wife, a former Peruvian film actress with great brown eyes, shoulder-length black hair, and a classic, high-cheekboned face. Her cool Latin beauty was intimidating. Yet she was gracious and friendly, and, I thought, a little mysterious. I liked her immediately, but even as we became friends over the years, I never knew just what was going on behind those lovely dark eyes.

Those first few days anchored off La Paz went by quickly as Duke settled into a shipboard routine of playing cards, snoozing, swimming, reading and drinking. (At this time Duke was partial to brandy on the rocks, although in later years he switched almost exclusively to tequila.)

Mostly, though, he played cards, usually with Pilar, but in a pinch with anyone aboard ship he could rope into a game of bridge or gin rummy. He was a sharp card player, having honed his skills during thirty-five years spent on movie sets killing time between camera setups. He was also a great chess fan. He was always ready for a game. Over the years Duke managed to humiliate a long line of crew members who thought they could take him on the chessboard. I had no such illusions, although I'd played the game as a boy. During later voyages I'd occasionally join him in a quick match. And I mean quick. He would beat me decisively. Finally, due to either pity or lack of challenge, he stopped asking me to play altogether.

Duke had proved something of a surprise to me. Easygoing, considerate, he didn't fit the mold of temperamental, demanding movie star. Nor did he seem overly fixated on himself. For one thing, he wasn't the least self-conscious about his baldness. He made no attempt to hide his lack of growth with a hat or wig while aboard ship. He didn't care if you took his picture sans hair. He was completely natural. And yet, bald or not, I found it hard not to sneak looks at him as I went about my chores. I never

UPPER: PILAR PALLETE ON THE SET OF *THE SEA CHASE* FILMING IN HAWAII SHORTLY BEFORE HER 1954 MARRIAGE TO DUKE. *BOB WILLOUGHBY PHOTO*

RIGHT: DUKE INDULGES IN HIS LOVE OF CHESS WHILE WAITING BETWEEN FILM SCENES. *PHIL STERN PHOTO*

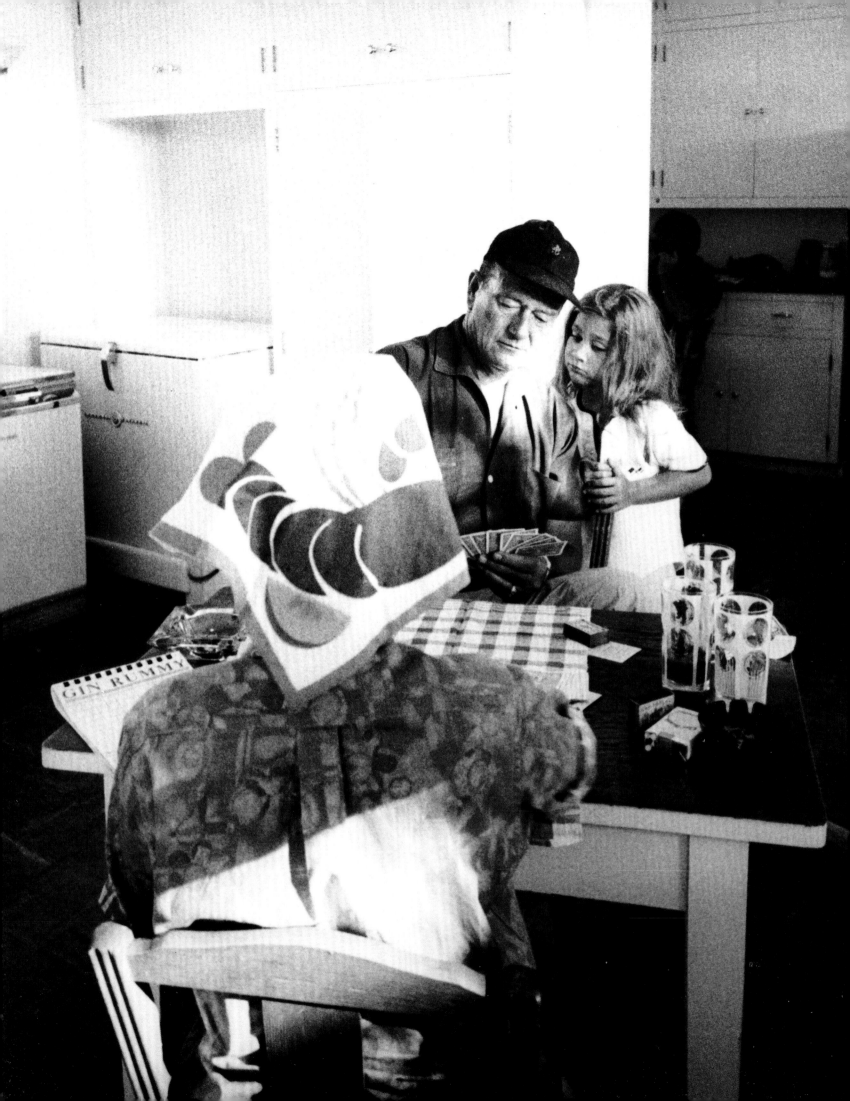

completely got over the urge to stare, even after we'd spent more than a decade together. I didn't consider myself prone to hero worship. And at the time I knew next to nothing about his screen roles. Yet for all his low-key ways, the impact of his personality was undeniable.

One evening, as Pete conducted his nightly bull session in the galley after dinner, Duke unexpectedly joined us. It was a habit he would repeat many times in the years ahead, pouring a cup of coffee and plopping down in any available chair. He seemed genuinely to enjoy the crew's company, and obviously got a kick out of the barrage of lies and exaggerations that we routinely tossed at each other like verbal grenades. He was especially attentive to Pete's special brand of inflated musings.

Tonight, as Pete was wrapping up a skin-crawling account of his days piloting banana boats from Central America to Newport Beach during World War II, Duke entered the galley and pulled up a chair.

"You had to be extra careful handling those bananas," Pete was saying, his rich baritone dropping to a near whisper as Duke settled in. "Tarantulas would hide in the bunches. You'd pick up a bunch, and one of the monsters would drop out on you. Hell of a thing to get a tarantula down your neck."

First mate Eduardo squirmed in his seat as he imagined the big spiders getting intimate. He admired Pete and believed him utterly in all things. Duke just grinned.

"Seems to me I heard about those tarantulas somewhere before," he said, looking sideways at Pete. "Aren't those the same tarantulas you told me about in the Bahamas on our way over to Spain?" Pete only grunted.

Duke reached for the open pack of cigarettes lying on the table in front of the skipper. Both men were heavy smokers, always puffing on a cigarette. It seemed as if I spent half my time emptying ashtrays after them.

Talk went on for at least an hour that night. Mostly between Pete and Duke. Toward the end Pete told a story about a cook he'd hired when he was skipper of another large yacht. The boat was set to sail for Mexico in a few days when Pete realized that the cook had yet to get any food aboard.

"There wasn't one crust of bread, not one bean, nothing," he recalled, warming to the tale. "So I ask the cook when he's going to get some food aboard. He tells me, 'Don't worry, Skipper. I'll take care of it.'

"So another day passes. Still no food. I ask him where's the food? Again he says, 'No problem. Leave it to me.' Well, this goes on until the day before we're due to shove off. Finally, I tell him to get the goddamn food aboard or start walking. He says, cool as you please, 'It's okay, Pete. It'll be here today.'

"Well, before long a refrigerated truck pulls up at the berth and the driver starts unloading stack after stack of cardboard boxes on the dock. I was so happy to see that stuff, I signed for the load without even reading the invoice. It wasn't until the guy drove away that I bothered to look at the receipt."

Pete paused for dramatic effect.

"Wouldn't you know it. I'd just signed for five hundred frozen TV dinners!"

Duke slapped his hand on the table and roared with laughter. Years later, after the skipper's death, he would muse how "ol' Pete" should've been an actor. He wondered how Pete might have taken to the idea. "I wish I'd gotten him into a couple of my movies," he'd say, a genuine note of regret in his voice. "He'd have been a natural."

•

ANOTHER ROUND OF CARDS WITH
DEAN MARTIN (LEFT), PILAR AND
FRIENDS. *GLOBE PHOTOS*

DUKE AND PILAR PLANNED TO ACCOMPANY THE BOAT UP THE MEXICAN COAST TO HER new home port at Newport Beach. Along the way, however, Duke was determined to get in as much fun as possible. At our first stop at Coyote Bay, about halfway between La Paz and Cabo San Lucas, he announced he was going waterskiing.

When I think back on that afternoon, I'm reminded of a scene from Duke's 1963 movie *Donovan's Reef*, directed by his friend and mentor, John Ford. In it the actor enjoys a good laugh at the expense of his pretty co-star, Elizabeth Allen. Duke's character, Guns Donovan, is driving a small speedboat around a tropical lagoon as Miss Allen waterskis behind. All is going well when Duke suddenly runs her up the ramp of a ski jump. She does a neat crash dive and comes up sputtering lagoon water. Duke is delighted at the soggy result.

Today, however, the laughs would all be on him. Privately, Pete doubted that the *Goose*'s tender, a seventeen-foot Boston Whaler powered by a fifty-five-horsepower outboard motor, had the guts to pull a man Duke's size from the water.

"It'll be like trying to pry a tree stump outta the ground using a can opener," he growled, ever the optimist.

As it turned out, he wasn't far wrong. Duke, strapped into a yellow flotation vest, oversized skis on his feet and a determined set to his jaw, ended up being dragged around Coyote Bay as much under the water as on top of it. As the skiboat's spotter, I was a firsthand witness to his difficulty in overcoming the laws of physics. Each time Pete hit the Whaler's throttle, Duke would disappear in a frothing cataract as the small boat strained to pick up speed. When the force became too great, the towrope would pop from his grasp like a giant rubber band, and he'd pitch headfirst into the Whaler's wake.

After several unsuccessful attempts, a chorus of support rose from crew members lining the *Goose*'s afterdeck gunwale. They were having a wonderful time—at Duke's expense.

Finally, Duke held on long enough for the Whaler to pull him up. Just like that, he was skiing. A large grin broke over his face as we circled the yacht. Suddenly, he let out a rebel yell: "YEAAAAAHOUEYYYYY!"

Everyone aboard the *Goose*—including Pilar, looking chic in sunglasses and a floppy straw hat—was clapping and cheering. It was a grand moment.

We made several circuits of the bay. It wasn't long, though, before Duke had had enough. He signaled to head back to the *Goose*. As we crossed the yacht's stern, he let loose of the towrope, sinking quickly in the calm water.

He was already sitting on the swim platform, dripping wet and smoking a cigarette, when we pulled up. He was breathing heavily, really quite winded, when a coughing attack came over him. He'd been coughing a lot since coming aboard. I didn't pay much attention to it. Probably just saltwater he had swallowed. And perhaps all those cigarettes he smoked.

The coughing subsided. Duke, breathing easier now, flicked the cigarette into the water, where it hissed out. "God," he said, shaking his head. "It's awful to grow old."

He would never try waterskiing again.

•

THE JUTTING, JAGGED ROCK FORMATIONS THAT DOMINATE CABO SAN LUCAS MARK THE tortured end of the eight-hundred-mile-long Baja peninsula. It was here a few days later

WATERSKIING OFF ACAPULCO. *PHIL STERN PHOTO*

that Pete Stein nearly skewered the *Goose* when we drifted into the bowsprit of a large schooner called the *Goodwill* while attempting to take on fresh water. Luckily for Pete, who had been drinking a little too much "coffee" that day, Duke and Pilar had taken the children in the Whaler up the coast fishing and so missed the excitement.

The *Goose*, as well as the schooner, escaped major damage, although Ken had to perform emergency surgery with a welding torch to reattach a section of metal railing torn loose from the *Goose*'s upper deck. Then a fresh coat of black paint and all was well. We said nothing to Duke about the incident on his return to the boat. And so went another day in the seagoing life of Captain Pete Stein.

Duke wanted to spend a while longer in the Cabo area before starting the return trip to Newport Beach. He knew some friends who owned a hotel a half-dozen miles back up the coast at a little resort town called Palmilla. Duke said we'd lay over there for a day or so. I didn't care. I was having the time of my life. This trip could go on forever, as far as I was concerned.

But it wouldn't. For tragedy was awaiting us in the dark waters off Palmilla.

A Tragic Night

It was Saturday night and the natives were restless aboard the *Wild Goose*. During our earlier stopover at Cabo, Daly Davies had got wind of a big fiesta to be held that evening at the cape. Joined by fellow party animals Eduardo, Raul and Efrem (son of Duke's valet, Fausto), Daly asked permission of Captain Stein to attend. Pete said okay, but he refused their request to sail back to the cape in the small skiff we used for short trips into shore. The craft was too unstable for a long haul in choppy water. They could instead get a taxi in Palmilla and cover the half-dozen miles by land.

I had planned to go along but at the last minute decided to stay aboard and catch up on some reading. I watched in the glare of the decklights as the four boys climbed into the skiff from the boarding ladder for the trip into shore. The skiff was little more than a glorified rowboat, about a dozen feet long, made of light plywood and powered by a small outboard motor. I waved good-bye as they disappeared into the dark toward the glowing lights of Palmilla.

It was the last time I'd ever see three of my shipmates again.

•

THE NEXT MORNING WE AWOKE TO FIND THAT THE BOYS HAD FAILED TO RETURN DURING the night. We weren't overly alarmed. They might have partied a little too hard and decided to sleep it off and return to the boat after daylight. But by mid-morning, with no sign yet of Daly and crew, Pete was worried.

"I hope they didn't take the skiff all the way to the cape," he kept saying. Finally, we decided we'd better see if we could find them.

Pete had already informed Duke of the boys' absence. He agreed that we should start a search immediately and volunteered to stay by the radio while we were gone. As Pete and I raced off in the Boston Whaler, I scanned the horizon and shoreline with binoculars. But there was no sign of the skiff or the boys.

At Cabo San Lucas we made the rounds of a small flotilla of private yachts anchored in the bay, asking if anyone had seen our missing shipmates. We drew a blank until one bleary-eyed American aboard a large motor sailer told us that he'd run into some lads at the fiesta the night before who said they worked for John Wayne aboard his private yacht. They left about midnight the same way they'd arrived, he said, yawning . . . in a small, open boat.

A chill went through me when I heard that. So they had taken the skiff to the fiesta against Pete's orders. There was little we could do except notify the local authorities, who told us a search by plane would begin within the hour. It was like a nightmare unfolding. Pete and I headed back to the *Wild Goose* with a feeling of increasing dread.

The next few hours were tough, as we monitored the radio. Then we heard it. A small craft had been found by a private sportfishing yacht. But what about the boys? The radio crackled that the sportfisher had taken aboard a sole survivor. It was Efrem, Fausto's son. There was no one else.

Our fears had been realized. When Efrem returned to the *Goose* a short time later, the lad was exhausted but otherwise in good shape. He was too tired to make much sense. But it was certain. The other boys were lost.

It wasn't until early the next morning, after Efrem had had a solid night's sleep, that we learned the entire, horrible story of that night aboard the skiff.

As Pete, Duke, Ken, Fausto and I gathered around him in the main salon, Efrem explained how the boys at the last minute had decided to ignore the skipper's instructions and instead take the skiff all the way to the cape to save taxi fare. Besides, they thought, it would be a nice little adventure.

The trip down was uneventful, and the boys spent a happy evening drinking tequila and dancing at the fiesta. Around midnight they piled in the skiff for the trip back. Efrem admitted that all four were tipsy.

It was a moonlit night, a strong breeze blowing and a little chill out on the water. Instead of hugging the curved shoreline, though, Eduardo decided they should cut across the open sea that lay between Palmilla and the cape to save some time. This maneuver put them several miles out in choppy water.

Raul, the steward, sitting in the exposed bow, soon complained about the cold spray coming over the gunwale. The others told him to move back to the boat's stern, out of the wet. In the dark, however, Raul tripped over a line in the skiff's bottom. He tried to regain his balance, but he tumbled overboard. The other boys jumped to help him. As they tried to drag him back aboard, however, the skiff suddenly flipped over, pitching them all into the sea. A serious emergency had turned into a disaster.

The boys fought to stay afloat in the rough water. They clung to the overturned skiff, gulping seawater as the waves broke over them. None wore life jackets. Their arms and legs began to ache as they strained to hold onto the bobbing skiff. They had no way of knowing just how much time had passed since the capsizing. Surely, thought the exhausted Efrem, it had to be hours.

Little Raul was the first to go. He told the others he could no longer hold on. He was going to try to reach shore. Eduardo, a good swimmer, tried to persuade the steward that he couldn't possibly make it. But Raul was too tired to listen. He let go and paddled out into the dark water. He didn't swim far before the boys saw him struggle and go under.

Eduardo immediately struck out in an attempt to save his shipmate. Efrem watched in the moonlight as the first mate repeatedly dove beneath the choppy surface. It was no use. Finally, the heroic Eduardo dove one last time. He did not reappear.

Now only Daly and Efrem were left clinging to the hull. With Daly's repeated encouragement, they managed to right the skiff, although it remained awash to the gunwales. They balanced themselves on the submerged seat as best they could. Daly spoke confidently that they would get out of this, doing his best to bolster Efrem's courage as well as his own, when a large wave struck the floundering boat and washed them clear. Efrem, stocky and strong, managed to grab onto the skiff's side. Daly, however, disappeared beneath the waves.

THE THREE DROWNED BOYS (FROM LEFT), RAUL, EDUARDO AND DALY DAVIES. *BERT MINSHALL PHOTO*

Efrem realized that he, too, would be swept away if he didn't do something soon. A nonswimmer, he knew the skiff was his only chance of survival. He managed to lash himself to the boat using the bowline. Then he waited through the night, alone on the sea.

It wasn't until mid-morning that he was spotted by the private sportfisher, *Dorsal*. (By coincidence, the *Dorsal* was owned by a good friend of Duke's, Elmer Hare, who would later be his cross-channel neighbor in Newport Beach.) Efrem had survived more than ten hours tied to the swamped skiff. His shipmates, however, were never found. It was presumed that the many sharks in those waters accounted for the absence of any bodies. An extra aspect of horror had been added to the tragedy.

Shock and sadness settled over us. Duke was visibly shaken.

"It just doesn't seem possible that we could lose three good men in one night," he said, shaking his head. Pete Stein wept openly.

The Waynes stayed largely to themselves during the next couple of days. Nerves were raw aboard ship. Once, Pete and Fausto fell into a bitter argument in the main salon. Pete had been very close to Eduardo. In his grief he accused Efrem of somehow being the cause of Eduardo's death. Perhaps the irony that Efrem, a nonswimmer, had survived while Eduardo, a strong swimmer, had not, proved too much for Pete. It seemed as if he and Fausto might come to blows when Pilar came to Fausto's defense, telling Pete he was out of line, that it was no one's fault. Things quieted down. Thankfully, there were no lingering hard feelings. Everyone realized that the blowup was due to the tension of the moment.

The leisurely voyage Duke had planned to Newport Beach was at an abrupt end. He and his family soon left the ship and flew by private plane to Los Angeles and their ranch home in nearby Encino. Fausto and Efrem went with them. Duke and Pilar sent condolences to the dead boys' families. Later, Pilar ordered Pete to get rid of the recovered skiff, saying she never wanted "to lay eyes on it again."

There were no immediate plans to hire replacements for the drowned crewmen. Pete, Ken, assistant engineer Tim and I would stand extra watches during the week-long voyage to San Diego, nine hundred miles north.

On our last day in that sad place we gathered topside for a brief memorial service. Pete ordered three flower wreaths specially made up from a local shop, one for each lad. Each bore the name *Wild Goose* and the names of our dead shipmates.

It was an overcast, cool morning as Pete read a few passages from the Bible. As he read I thought about what fine young men these three mates had been. Especially my friend Daly.

My mind went back to earlier that year to a storm we had run into while crossing the Gulf of Tehauntepec, near the Mexico-Guatemala border. It was about three in the morning and I had engine-room watch. To escape the heat and noise of the diesels, I'd gone topside for a few minutes, where I saw Daly sacked out on an afterdeck couch. Daly often complained about the stuffiness of crew's quarters and would retreat on many nights to the fresh air of the afterdeck. Now he was snoozing in his favorite spot, wedged firmly against the couch's back cushion as the big yacht rolled heavily in the mountainous swells.

As I was about to go back below, a huge wave slammed into the *Goose*, throwing me to my hands and knees. I heard the crash of breaking glass. Three starboard windows had given way under the tremendous force of the sea. I scrambled to my feet and steadied myself as a flood of cold water washed in through the windows and across the afterdeck, carrying chairs and cushions before it.

Poor Daly, asleep on the opposite couch, never knew what hit him. As the water from the rogue swell swept across the deck it rushed up and over the couch, drenching him. He nearly floated off with the surge. He struggled upright. But the ship heaved again, throwing him face first across the afterdeck's large poker table.

Sea spray was whipping in through the broken windows as I rushed to help him. It looked like a scene from *Victory at Sea*. Shards of broken glass were strewn about the slippery deck. I had to convince Daly that the bloody ship wasn't sinking.

"Jesus, Bert!" he shouted above the roar, soaked and shaken. "I thought I was a goner!"

We laughed about it at the time. Now, after the tragedy of the past week, the memory of that night came back to me. It seemed even then that the sea was reaching out for Daly. Well, I thought, it had finally got a grip on him. For good. And it got greedy and took two others as well.

MEMORIAL WREATHS IN HONOR OF THE *GOOSE*'S DEAD SHIPMATES. *BERT MINSHALL PHOTO*

Pete concluded the service and asked Ken and me to throw the wreaths, one at a time, into the sea. They floated together in a group before drifting apart. We could see them far out on the water for a long time.

"Okay, Ken," said Pete, still holding the Bible. "Let's get the hell out of here."

Crisis and Change

Duke planned a major renovation of the *Wild Goose* as soon as the boat was permanently berthed in Newport Beach. But in the fall of 1964 an unexpected medical crisis threatened to put not only an abrupt end to those plans, but to all Duke knew and loved in life. The crisis was lung cancer.

All that coughing aboard ship. All those cigarettes. At the time, everyone—including Duke—chalked it up to just a bad case of smoker's hack. But who knows? Perhaps even then the first rogue cancer cells had invaded his lungs.

Duke knew something was seriously wrong following the filming of *In Harm's Way*, a big-budget war picture he shot in Hawaii with director Otto Preminger not long after he left the *Goose*. Weeks later, after he'd returned from location to his home in Encino, outside Los Angeles, his cough had worsened. Even then, he later said, he could've ignored it. But when it comes to coughing up blood, even John Wayne can get scared.

Pilar finally persuaded her stubborn husband to see a doctor. The diagnosis was a stunner. A malignant growth the size of a golf ball had been detected on his left lung. Duke had cancer. Surgery would have to be immediate and drastic if he was to have any chance of survival.

DUKE, SMOKING EVER-PRESENT CIGARETTE, AND SON PATRICK ABOARD AN EARLIER WAYNE VESSEL, THE SEVENTY-FIVE-FOOT *NOR'WESTER*. PHIL STERN PHOTO

While all this was going on, the *Wild Goose* had spent a wonderful, relaxed sum-mer cruising the spectacular inland passages of British Columbia, fifteen hundred miles north of Newport Beach. The boat was under extended charter to Duke's good friend Max Wyman, Seattle lumber tycoon and the *Goose*'s previous owner. It was Max who had sold the big yacht to Duke in 1962 for $110,000.

The decision to charter the *Goose* was financially straightforward—she would be earning money while Duke was busy filming in Hawaii. Also, the yacht's Newport Beach berth was not yet available. Better to have her cruise through pristine wilderness—and get paid for it—than linger at dockside in San Diego with each day taking another bite out of Duke's pocketbook.

Toward the end of summer, while passing through a rock-studded passage called Dodd Narrows, about thirty miles north of Vancouver, Canada, the *Goose* drifted in the swift current and grounded against a rock outcropping. The stem was deeply gouged below the waterline, but luckily there was no serious flooding in the forward bilges. Max Wyman flew home to Seattle while we hauled out in Vancouver for repairs.

A simple patch job became a major restoration, however, when rotten hull planks were discovered adjoining the stem. An entire new bow would have to be installed to make the then twenty-year-old vessel seaworthy again.

In late September, as work progressed on the *Goose*, we first heard over the news that John Wayne had entered a Los Angeles hospital for surgery to correct an "ankle injury" he'd received when he pulled a tendon some years earlier. We were not unduly alarmed. If it was serious, we figured, Duke's office would have notified us. Yet, a few days later, with the actor still in the hospital and reportedly experiencing respiratory complications—from ankle surgery, of all things—we suspected something more sinis-ter than a tweaked tendon was wrong with our boss.

After a week without confirmed word on his condition, the rumors took off. Duke had had a heart attack, he was suffering from emphysema, pneumonia, cancer. Hell, some people said he had the plague. There were even reports that he was dead, and the hospital and family were involved in a massive coverup. Aboard the *Goose*, we simply went about our work and worried.

On October 8, 1964, after a three-week stay, Duke was discharged from Good Samaritan Hospital, about forty pounds lighter than when he went in, minus two ribs, a lung and part of another, but obviously alive and looking strikingly well under the circumstances. In December he confirmed what many had suspected—that he'd under-gone surgery for removal of a cancerous tumor. He went public, he said, in the hope that his example would persuade others to seek early diagnosis. He had beaten "the Big C," as he called it. He was proof that a diagnosis of cancer was not an automatic death sentence.

While Duke spoke to the press in Los Angeles, the *Wild Goose* was making her way down the Pacific coast. Repairs were complete, her bow totally replanked and a new stem installed. It had been a year and a half since she'd left the States bound for

Barcelona. Along the way she'd lost three of her own on a moonlit night off Baja. But she had also sailed a distance almost equal to a trip around the world, burned a staggering seventy-five thousand gallons of diesel fuel, crossed the Atlantic Ocean—twice— and made ports-of-call in eight different countries.

It was a sunny winter day when the *Wild Goose* finally eased her 287 tons into berth 54 at the Lido Yacht Anchorage in Newport Harbor. The mains shuddered to a stop, and Pete Stein stepped out on the bridge wingdeck to light a cigarette.

I looked back along the *Goose*'s white hull. The dock was one of the biggest in Newport, yet thirty feet of boat still stuck out into the channel. It would have to do. Berth 54 was now home.

•

NEWPORT HARBOR HAS CHANGED TREMENDOUSLY OVER THE YEARS. ONCE MUD FLATS and beach shacks, it's been dredged and developed into one of the world's most exclusive luxury harbors. Entire islands rise from the bay where none existed before. Long rows of expensive private yachts jam miles of moorings. To a lad who grew up around the bleak backwaters of Liverpool, Newport Harbor in early 1965 was nothing less than a seaside Xanadu.

Duke had chosen Newport, one of the haunts of his youth, as his new home. He bought a house overlooking the harbor in the exclusive Bayshore Drive area and began immediate remodeling. The *Wild Goose* was also to be put to hammer and saw. It was time the yacht was customized to reflect the needs and tastes of her owner.

As these projects got under way, our boss fought to regain his health. His incredible stamina—along with possibly a fair dose of bullheadedness—drove him on. He stunned his doctors with the speed and vigor of his recovery. Ignoring their protests, he flew to

DUKE WITH ETHAN, PILAR AND AISSA AT THEIR NEW BAYSHORE ESTATE IN NEWPORT BEACH DURING REMODELING. *BOB WILLOUGHBY PHOTO*

Durango, Mexico, to begin filming *The Sons of Katie Elder* with good friend Dean Martin. The mile-high location was tough on Duke's breathing. Some of the action scenes nearly did him in. But he gutted it out, determined to see it through.

His first visit dockside in Newport Beach he looked on the thin side, but his grip was strong and his movements solid. In fact, he radiated vitality—the enthusiasm, perhaps, of a man who has stood at death's door and had it slammed squarely in his face. He might be a bit worse for wear and tear, he laughed, but it sure as hell beat the alternative.

Remodeling on the *Goose* now began in earnest. Ceilings were raised six to eight inches to accommodate Duke's six-foot-four-inch height. A bulkhead was ripped out, nearly doubling the size of the main salon, which now came complete with woodburning fireplace, poker table and built-in wet bar. A spectacular mural of a seventeenth-century sea battle—painted by a movie-studio artist Duke hired—decorated the forward bulkhead.

The *Goose*'s exterior lines were transformed by construction of a new master stateroom aft of the wheelhouse. This comfortable compartment, which wrapped around the ship's smokestack, included separate quarters for Duke's children.

Built into the rear bulkhead of this stateroom and overlooking the *Goose*'s boatdeck (so-called because this large topside deck was where the yacht's tenders were stored when not in use) was the *hickea*—Hawaiian for couch, according to Duke. This sprawling lounge area was shaded by a red-and-white-striped canvas awning. Duke loved to play cards here or catch a snooze in the afternoon. It became one of his favorite shipboard spots.

Duke often drove the sixty miles from Encino to check the progress both aboard the *Goose* and at his Bayshore estate. Sometimes he and Pilar would spend the weekend aboard ship at dockside. After he sold the Encino property (reportedly to the oldest daughter of Walt Disney), he and his family moved into temporary quarters at the nearby Newporter Inn while they waited for work to conclude on their nine-thousand-square-foot, seven-bedroom home.

Ken and I performed most of the carpentry work during the early stages of the

Top: Bert Minshall varnishing the Goose's trim during re-modeling in Newport Beach.

Center: Work under way on the addition of a new master stateroom.

Lower: Finished stateroom, with Bert standing beside the *hickea*, destined to be one of Duke's favorite shipboard lounging areas. *Bert Minshall photos (3)*

Goose's remodeling. When we took over the afterdeck with our table saws and work benches, Duke jokingly accused us of turning the ship into a floating lumbermill. We were soon joined by five freelance marine carpenters. Duke would stand in the sawdust that covered the deck of our makeshift woodshop or perch on a stack of lumber while we worked. He seemed to get a kick out of all the action swirling about him.

Duke had hired an interior decorator to put together a design scheme for the main salon. One afternoon he listened impatiently as the decorator described his "vision" for the new compartment. That vision included ornate gold handles on cabinet doors and avocado-and-gold-foil wallpaper. Duke shook his head.

"Hell, no," he said, cutting the decorator off in mid-sentence. "I don't want my boat turned into a goddamned French whorehouse."

Duke was proud of his yacht and delighted in showing her off to friends. One day actress Maureen O'Hara was due aboard. The fiery redhead was probably Duke's most popular leading lady. She co-starred in some of his best films, including the John Ford classics *Rio Grande* and *The Quiet Man*. The actress and Duke were great friends.

Duke was drinking coffee in the ship's galley as he awaited Miss O'Hara's arrival. After a half-hour or so, all that coffee overloaded his personal plumbing, and he excused himself to make a quick trip to the crew's head.

"Keep a lookout for Miss O'Hara while I'm gone," he drawled as he ducked out the door.

He wasn't gone thirty seconds when I heard footsteps coming up the dock. I jumped to the gunwale and saw a lovely redhead peering up at the yacht. What timing, I thought. Maureen O'Hara had arrived just as Duke was answering the call of nature. I rushed down the boarding steps to greet her. In my enthusiasm, however, I let tact go flying in the sea breeze.

"Hello, Miss O'Hara!" I shouted, hurrying forward. The actress smiled. "Mr. Wayne will be right with you. He's in the toilet."

Her smile vanished into a look of genuine surprise.

"Oh!" she gasped. "You didn't have to tell me that!"

For all the changes taking place aboard the *Goose*, including installation of sophisticated navigation equipment, Duke insisted that as much of her navy heritage be preserved as possible. Old-fashioned wall fans on swivel mounts still swept the crew's quarters and the galley as they had in the ship's days as a minesweeper during World War II. Secured on the foredeck was the original ship's bell, the letters "USN" engraved on its polished brass face. In the wheelhouse, arrayed against an aft bulkhead, was the ship's first on-board communications system—a row of brass-tipped speaking tubes. A drum-shaped enunciator, or telegraph, its brass handles used for signaling FLANK, REVERSE, HALF-SPEED and so forth, relayed bell-clanging engine room commands through a system of pulleys and chains. (Although there were automatic engine controls in the wheelhouse, Duke nonetheless wanted the enunciator equipment kept in good working order.)

The pride of the wheelhouse was the ship's large, brass-rimmed helm. Pete had issued standing orders that no one was to touch the brass rim (we steered, when not on automatic pilot, using the wheel's painted iron center spokes). He cringed every time Duke ambled up to the helm, knowing he'd invariably grab hold of the brass, leaving smears and fingerprints behind.

Even the decks of the *Goose* were painted navy gray, as was the trim work. She was

DUKE POINTS FROM OUTSIDE THE WHEELHOUSE AS ETHAN AND AISSA PLAY BY THE GOOSE'S ORIGINAL NAVY BRASS HELM. *PHIL STERN PHOTO*

still the same brilliant, white-hulled vessel she was when I joined her in Barcelona, but with her massive, functional navy lines she stood out like a lumberjack at a debutante ball among the glossy sleekness of many of Newport's more modern yachts. And that was just the way Duke liked it.

Practically speaking, the *Goose* was a miniature sea-going city. Three generators and a large bank of batteries provided electricity to dozens of outlets and lights plus all the ship's electronic navigation equipment. In the engine room was a complete machine shop for emergency repairs and routine maintenance. Ten thousand gallons of diesel fuel gave the ship a cruising range of well over three thousand miles. More than three thousand gallons of fresh water was stored in two tanks, while two watermakers could produce an additional forty gallons an hour. There were miles of electrical wiring and piping throughout the ship.

Ken always insisted that the engine room was the real heart of the *Goose*—and it was a navy heart that thundered to the roar of two giant GMC eight-cylinder diesels. Duke didn't visit the engine room often, but when he did, he was fascinated. Here was history that lived and worked, hardly changed since the ship's tour of duty in the navy, when she was stationed in the Aleutian Islands, off Alaska. Duke loved it.

This navy fixation may have had something to do with Duke's hope when growing up of making the service a career. He even applied to the U.S. Naval Academy at Annapolis, but was turned down. Fifty years later, with all the acclaim of being the world's biggest film star, he still called his failure to attend Annapolis "one of the greatest disappointments of my life."

LEFT: WITH LANA TURNER IN *THE SEA CHASE*.

LOWER: DUKE GETS THE POINT FROM A MUTINOUS CREW IN *ADVENTURE'S END*, 1937.

RIGHT: SURVIVING A CAPSIZING IN A SPECTACULAR SCENE FROM *CIRCUS WORLD*. PHOTOFEST (3)

Duke's fans sometimes fail to realize just how often he appeared in films with navy or nautical themes. No fewer than fifteen of his films were set on the sea, or at least used it as background. As early as 1930 he appeared as a sailor trapped in a submarine in *Men Without Women*, directed by John Ford and shot in the waters off Catalina. The year following his big break in *Stagecoach* he appeared in another big-budget Ford film, *The Long Voyage Home*, in which he played a Swedish sailor.

In his navy pictures he commanded everything from PT boats to heavy cruisers. He was also a naval aviator, a Seabee, as well as skipper of a U.S. Coast Guard cutter chasing poachers and smugglers.

I think Duke is best known, though, for his lone-wolf roles, usually portraying a tough sea captain on some seemingly impossible, or even outlaw, voyage—pictures like *Wake of the Red Witch* with Gail Russell, or *The Sea Chase*, where Duke commands a German freighter with a cargo full of Lana Turner.

And though he spends most of his time on land under a bigtop in *Circus World*, one of his most spectacular water scenes takes place in that movie, when a freighter capsizes at its pier. Fans may not recall much else about the film, but they seldom forget the sight of that big ship keeling over.

Duke's sea films, together with his love of the *Wild Goose*'s naval heritage and his early longing to attend Annapolis, say something important about my boss. Although Duke will forever be synonymous with the American West, he was really a sailor at heart.

Recovery

I t would take six months to complete remodeling aboard the *Wild Goose*. By that time Duke and his family had moved into their new estate at 2686 Bayshore Drive. Newport Beach was now officially home.

The summer of 1965 was a time of continued recovery and readjustment for Duke. To help his breathing he was forced to undergo periodic oxygen treatments. During this time we made several weekend cruises aboard the *Goose* to Santa Catalina Island, twenty-seven miles off the Newport Harbor breakwater. Duke would bring with him his oxygen bottle and breathing mask, which he kept ready in his stateroom. He hated using the equipment. He hated looking like an invalid.

He had no such qualms, though, about showing off his operation scar—and it was a hell of a sight. He'd come out on the boatdeck in his swim trunks, oblivious to the jagged white line of raised tissue that started under his left arm and ran down across his chest. Duke's torso looked as if it were held together by a giant zipper.

His main postoperative gripe centered on his continued difficulty in breathing. While filming *The Sons of Katie Elder* in the Mexican high desert he said he was constantly struggling to catch his breath. Even aboard the *Goose* he was often gasping. And his coughing attacks were truly horrendous as he fought to clear the thick mucus from his one remaining lung. But altitude was the real killer, he complained.

(A year later, when Walt Disney, creator of Mickey Mouse and Disneyland, lost a lung to cancer, Duke sent a telegram that read: "WELCOME TO THE CLUB. THE ONLY PROBLEM IS HEIGHT. DUKE.")

Height, however, wasn't the only problem facing a man with one lung, as Duke found out later that summer during a scuba-diving expedition to San Nicklas Island, about fifty miles from Catalina. An old hand at snorkeling and diving, he was enthusiastic about going after the succulent abalone and lobster that populate the San Nicklas reefs.

On our arrival I was recruited to join Duke as his diving partner. At the time I protested that I knew nothing about diving, but Duke only grinned and said, "You'll learn or drown tryin'." After a quick tutorial on the ship's gently swaying swim platform, he pronounced me ready to conquer the depths. He gripped my mask, checking to see if it was on tight. For a moment all I could see was his huge palm covering the glass.

"Okay, just stay calm and breathe easy," he said, satisfied. I stepped off the platform and sank into another world.

It was exhilarating . . . and a little intimidating. The water was strikingly clear. I could easily see the *Goose*'s twin propellers looming before me. But when I tried to dive deeper, a piercing pain shot through my ears. Duke had warned me about the potentially painful effects of water pressure. I tried to equalize the pressure by pinching my nose and blowing, as he had showed me. But the pain continued. It was excruciating. Disappointed, I swam back to the surface.

Meanwhile, Duke was having his own problems. With only one lung, he couldn't get enough oxygen through his regulator to offset the exertion of diving. It wasn't long before he shot back to the surface, gasping for air.

He made another attempt after he'd regained his breath, but it was no use. His lack of lung power again forced him to surface after just a few minutes. He ripped the big triangular diving mask from his face and flung it onto the *Goose*'s swim platform.

"Goddamnit!" he swore loudly, coughing and fighting for air. "I'll never have any more fun!"

The frustration showed clearly in his face. Heaving his fins ahead of him, he climbed the aluminum sea ladder. Having already slipped out of my gear, I helped him off with his tank and weight belt. He didn't say anything as he squeezed by me on the narrow platform. He was still dripping water, as he went up the transom ladder to the enclosed afterdeck.

Later that evening, Duke joined the crew for a cup of coffee as we ate dinner in the galley. After a few minutes of small talk, he grew silent. Suddenly, he slammed his coffee cup on the table and glared at me.

"And you!" he growled, real anger in his voice. "You white-toothed bastard! You wouldn't even go down. Why didn't you go deeper?"

DUKE ENDED UP WITH AN EAR INFECTION DOING SCENES LIKE THIS ONE IN *WAKE OF THE RED WITCH*. *PHOTOFEST*

Everyone stopped eating. I guess it must have seemed grossly unfair to him that I, only thirty-two years old and vibrantly healthy, apparently wouldn't dive, while he, who so very much wanted to, couldn't due to the loss of his lung.

All eyes were on me. I stammered something about wanting to dive deeper, then attempted to explain the problem with my ears.

Duke listened, then pushed back in his chair.

"Yeah, I know what you mean," he said, the anger gone as quickly as it had come. "I picked up a fungus infection in my ears doing the diving scenes in *Wake of the Red Witch*. Whenever I go swimming it bothers me."

He looked out the galley's open door toward San Nicklas, growing dark against the horizon. It was a lovely late-summer evening.

"Ah, what the hell," he said, picking up his coffee cup once more. "I've had a lot of fun diving over the years. It's too bad your ears can't take it. You don't know what you're missing."

That day off San Nicklas was the last time he would attempt the sport. The physical limitations of having only one lung were indeed real, even for a man of Duke's monumental determination. From now on, he would learn to live with such disappointments.

And yet, Duke also knew he had much to be thankful for. He'd recovered as well as any man could following his bout with cancer, his marriage to Pilar seemed to be going well, and his children were young enough to make cruises aboard ship family affairs. The conditions would never again be so right for him to fully enjoy the aging minesweeper. The middle to late sixties were really the *Wild Goose*'s Pacific glory years.

Duke had intended to use the yacht as a floating retreat while he filmed movies on location. But because many of his films were shot in and around Durango, Mexico, 150 miles inland, the logistics of getting to the coast and back proved unworkable. Only when he made *McQ* in Seattle, Washington, in 1973, did he manage to stay aboard during filming.

So, instead of a floating dressing room, the yacht served as movable playground between films. We began a cycle of seasonal cruising between Mexico and the Pacific Northwest, sailing south in the winter, north in the summer. Duke was usually far too busy to join the boat for an entire voyage (one year alone we spent five straight months cruising off Mexico), but when free he'd fly in by private plane to wherever the ship might be, stay a few days or a few weeks, then fly back to California. He sometimes made three or four round trips in this way during the course of a long voyage.

That fall Duke ordered the *Wild Goose* south to Acapulco, where he later joined us for several weeks. At this time the great event in his life was the unexpected—yet happy—news that Pilar was pregnant. Duke was fifty-eight and thrilled at the prospect of having another child. I remember how Pilar brought aboard a variety of food supplements as a boost to her diet during this time. Bottles and bags of vitamins, yeast and protein were strewn about the galley. It looked like a seagoing health-food store.

(On February 22, 1966, Pilar gave birth to the couple's third child, Marisa Carmela Wayne. Little more than a year after his near-fatal brush with cancer, Duke became a father for the seventh and last time.)

We spent several weeks docked at the Club de Yates in Acapulco. Duke loved the Mexican resort city—even though the humidity and heat could wilt iron. Before he bought the *Goose* he'd acquired a half-interest in a mansion overlooking the city. The

DUKE LOOKS OVER A PARROT WHILE SHOPPING IN ACAPULCO. *PHIL STERN PHOTO*

DUKE AT THE WHEEL OF HIS STATION
WAGON WITH MARISA (BEING HELD
BY HER NANNY), ON THE WAY HOME
FROM THE BABY'S CHRISTENING.
BERNIE ABRAMSON PHOTO

LEFT: PILAR LIFTING WEIGHTS TO STRENGTHEN HER TENNIS GAME. *BERT MINSHALL PHOTO*

RIGHT: A HOME-MOVIE SEQUENCE OF DUKE WORKING THROUGH A SET ON THE GOOSE'S BOATDECK. *BERT MINSHALL FILM (3)*

brilliant white estate sat on a cliff of red volcanic rock high above the Pacific.

As the years went by, however, Duke grew increasingly uncomfortable using the house. He complained that there were "always too many people around"—meaning guests invited by the other owner. Nor did Duke care much for his partner's girlfriend's three wonderfully useless felines—Mamba, Samba and Cha-Cha—who were fixtures on the patio. Duke quietly resented this invasion of his privacy, both human and cat. He kept the house as an investment, but on later trips south usually chose to stay aboard ship . . . and "away from those damn cats."

During our stay at the Club de Yates, I talked Duke into lifting weights with me in the mornings.

I'd always been a big believer in the benefits of exercise, especially weight training. I kept a few barbells and dumbbells aboard that I used to keep in shape.

As Duke watched me going through my paces, I suggested he join me in my morning workouts. Although I didn't think he'd take me up on it, I told him that I'd be happy to set up a program for him. Duke seemed interested.

"Could you figure out something to help my breathing?" he asked. I said I'd see what I could do, though still not convinced he'd actually follow through.

But when I dragged my weights out the next morning, Duke strolled on deck wearing a pair of red swim trunks, ready to begin work. He must have weighed close to 260. He could really pack on the pounds between pictures.

I showed him several exercises, alternating sets so he could see my form and rhythm. I started him out with light squats, overhead presses, upright rowing, arm curls and knee lifts (which he performed while sitting on the edge of the *hickea*). On the overhead presses the bar wobbled so much I thought he was going to lose his balance and fall over backward.

But he toiled and strained through the exercises, determined to see the torture through. For the next few weeks he continued to join me every other morning for a workout. He seldom missed a session, although after that first morning he said he was so sore he felt as though someone had beat him with a club.

At Duke's insistence I became his personal taskmaster.

"C'mon, Bert," he'd hiss between clenched teeth as he did his repetitions, "make me keep doing it so it will help my breathing." Even Pilar got caught up in the sweaty spirit, exercising her arms lightly to strengthen her tennis game.

At the end of three weeks the results were noticeable—Duke had shed fifteen pounds, his breathing came easier and his muscle tone improved. He was pleased and said he planned to keep lifting when he returned to Newport Beach.

On his return home, however, his passion for pumping iron soon cooled (although on later voyages he would still occasionally join me in a workout). He had a small gym with weights set up at his home, but they saw little use. Without someone to push him, he lost interest.

He didn't abandon all exercise, though. He still went on his early morning walks around Bayshore. He moved at a good clip, eating up ground with his great strides. He said no one really bothered him during these walks, although he admitted it was odd how at least one woman always seemed to choose the exact moment he was puffing by her home to step out and retrieve the morning paper.

"She must see me coming through her binoculars," he said, only half-joking.

A Seagoing Feast

That first year in Newport the *Wild Goose* acquired a new crew member. Billy Sweatt stood only five-foot-four, but he was a giant in the galley. Duke liked to boast that "No crew's gonna eat better than the *Wild Goose's*!" For twelve years Billy made good on that promise.

Billy was from North Carolina, a quarter Cherokee Indian, black-haired with smoky-black eyes, thirty-eight years old when he joined the *Goose*. He once dreamed of being a professional jockey until he suffered a career-ending injury in a fall from a mount. His restless spirit and a love of cooking eventually led him to Newport Beach and a new career as a freelance seacook. By the time Duke hired him, Billy's reputation for galley wizardry was solid. Duke wanted the best, and to him, Billy was it.

Between 1965 and 1977, when he became too sick from emphysema to continue his duties, Billy looked after the gastronomic well-being of Duke, his family, guests and crew. Dieters soon abandoned all hope of counting calories while under the culinary care of Billy Sweatt. His shipboard spreads became legendary around Newport Beach. For example, a typical day's menu would begin with a breakfast of cantaloupe, grapefruit, pancakes, bacon and sausage, fruit juices, milk, eggs (any style and as many as you'd want), muffins and toast.

If you survived breakfast, your digestive system would get a reprieve until lunch, when Billy might produce a platter of hamburgers with all the fixings, accompanied by heaped trays of green onions, cut celery and carrots, iced cauliflower, potato chips and more glasses of cold milk. Or, if guests and crew were in the middle of a hard day of swimming and sunbathing, he might simply leave out a plate piled with cold cuts and sliced cheeses, a couple of loaves of bread and a condiment tray, with instructions for all aboard—and that included Duke—to dig in for themselves.

SHIP'S COOK, BILLY SWEATT, CARVES A CHRISTMAS TURKEY ON THE AFTERDECK. *BERT MINSHALL PHOTO*

But dinner was the day's main caloric event . . . thick New York steaks, huge baked potatoes drowning in gravy or sour cream, string beans cooked with baby onions, steamed artichoke hearts, hot rolls, more milk, nearly always a good table wine, and a dessert of deep-dish apple pie baked that morning, topped with slabs of Neapolitan ice cream. Billy was a man who didn't know the meaning of the word cholesterol. No wonder I would gain ten pounds after a long cruise.

BILLY WITH DINNER—FRESH ALASKAN KING CRAB. *BERT MINSHALL PHOTO*

Billy routinely put in fourteen-hour days preparing these shipboard feasts, rising at five to begin breakfast and to plan the day's menu. The ship's steward assisted him in his work, serving meals, handling cleanup and helping with simple cooking chores. The *Goose* traditionally experienced a high turnover in stewards . . . Billy worked most of them into early retirement.

Like skipper Pete Stein, Billy was partial to scotch whisky. It may sound extravagant, but normally after breakfast Billy would pour his first scotch-and-water of the day. Billy's capacity for drink was out of all proportion to his size—he could put it away like a burly stevedore.

In the late 1960s a film production company hired the *Goose* as a floating prop for the movie *Skidoo*, starring comedian Jackie Gleason. One morning during a lull in filming, Billy invited the funnyman to join him in a drink. Gleason, a man of both legendary size and thirst, accepted . . . happily. Billy poured a hefty tumbler and watched in admiration as Gleason smacked his lips, rolled his eyes and gulped bloody near half the glass in one swallow. "God, that's beautiful," sighed the comedian. Then the two men settled down to an hour of conversation, accompanied, of course, by more scotch.

Later Billy prepared a delicious dinner of chicken and dumplings. The scotch seemed to serve as a lubricant to keep him functioning smoothly throughout the day. He explained it to me once. "It's a formula, Bert," he said in his slightly nasal, though pleasant, voice. "So many parts booze to so many hours work. Most people get those two things out of balance, and then they're in trouble. Pacing is the key. Keep to the pace, Bert. Just keep to the pace."

After Billy left the ship Duke employed a cook who paced himself on his drinking about as well as a man running downhill. One night, while preparing dinner in a scotch haze, he set Duke's pork chops afire. He rescued them from the oven through a billowing cloud of smoke. They were burnt black. He tried scraping away the carbon crust but finally gave up and served them as is. Duke grimly chewed his blowtorched chops like a bulldog biting through its leather leash, but he didn't complain. It wouldn't have done any good. The cook had disappeared below decks, where he had the disconcerting habit of smoking in his bunk. After a hard day in the galley, he would turn out the lights and contemplate the world, the red tip of his cigar glowing ominously in the dark.

•

Trips to Mexico meant lobster. Lots of lobster. We'd trade with the local fishermen for dozens of the creatures at a time, bartering everything from cartons of cigarettes and bottles of Cutty Sark scotch to Duke's old clothes. Back issues of *Playboy* magazine were always good for several bags of meaty tails. Duke would joke that we could wipe out the lobster population of Baja California if we could only get our hands on enough old *Playboys* to trade. He used to tell us to "get the literature out"—meaning the *Playboys*—whenever he saw the fishermen sailing up to the yacht in their small boats.

During one southern cruise we stockpiled more than five hundred lobster tails in the ship's huge walk-in freezer, located directly below the galley in the ship's pantry. To seal in freshness, we'd freeze the meat in empty milk cartons filled with water.

At times we traded for whole lobsters. Duke would sometimes help bring the creatures aboard, laying them on the deck as they were handed up to him from the stern. There'd be as many as a half-dozen wet lobsters crawling about.

"Whoa there!" he'd laugh as we scurried after the wandering crustaceans. "Let's round 'em up!" He sounded as if he were riding herd on a cattle drive along the Chisholm Trail, not conducting a lobster chase on the *Wild Goose*'s afterdeck. He liked to tease little Marisa by holding a wriggling lobster in each hand and slowly advancing on her as she giggled and hid behind my legs.

One of Duke's favorite dishes was Shrimp Cannles, named after his friend Seattle restaurateur Peter Cannles. Billy would cook the shrimp in their shells in a giant cast-iron skillet, adding wine and mounds of garlic salt and spices as they simmered. Duke liked to suck the juice from the shells before eating the delicious meat. He could, and did, consume dozens of shrimp at a sitting. His appetite for shrimp was voracious.

He was also a fanatic for grapefruit. He could devour one or two whole ones with his breakfast. He ate everything except the rind, scraping the insides clean. I, too, liked grapefruit and made the mistake one morning at breakfast of saying so. Duke, seated across from me, reared back in his chair.

"You don't like 'em as much as I do!" he bellowed.

Duke put on weight easily, sometimes ballooning to 250 or 260 pounds. If he had a movie coming up, he'd use his time aboard ship to diet and exercise in hopes of getting down to what he considered his best working weight of around 230. But if he'd just finished a film, Duke didn't seem to care how many notches he added to his belt.

During the mid-1960s there was a deckhand aboard the *Goose* who weighed well over 300 pounds. Fat Ernie Foster (his own nickname), was a good seaman and was well liked by Duke and his shipmates, but his girth was so great he could barely fit through the yacht's narrow doorways. One afternoon while the *Goose* was anchored off Catalina, Duke persuaded Fat Ernie to have a go at waterskiing. "If the Whaler can get

Trading *Playboy* magazines for fresh lobster in Mexico. *Bert Minshall photo* me up, it can get you up," Duke told him. Someone should have told the Whaler.

We thought the small craft's motor would melt under the strain of trying to pull the colossal crewman from the water. We dragged poor Ernie around the *Goose* like a barge full of coal. Duke finally called off the attempt, afraid the towrope would snap.

The quantity of food Fat Ernie routinely put away was astonishing. At one sitting he could demolish a dozen large pancakes, an equal number of sausages and a huge plate of scrambled eggs. One evening as a joke we piled a half-dozen New York steaks on Ernie's dinner plate. Ernie, his knife and fork at the ready, stared at the mound of meat before him. Just then, Duke entered the galley. He did a double take when he saw Fat Ernie's plate. "Good God!" he gasped. "It'd pay me to keep you at home!"

•

IT WAS TRADITIONAL ABOARD THE *WILD GOOSE* THAT THE CREW EAT FIRST. THIS WAS largely a case of efficiency. We ate quickly and were soon back to our duties, leaving the Waynes and any shipboard guests to enjoy a leisurely dinner on the afterdeck. Always, though, we shared the same menu.

Duke used to enjoy barbecues aboard ship. Billy would set up a grill on the boatdeck, charbroiling steaks, or fish that Duke had caught earlier that day. If the barbecuing took place up north, there'd be a few chunks of salmon fillet sizzling on the grill.

Duke loved to catch and eat salmon, but he drew the line at cleaning them. That task usually fell to Billy and me. We'd fillet the huge fish (some weighed up to forty pounds) on the afterdeck, working on a cutting board set up with running water on the gunwale. We'd load up the ship's freezer with dozens of fillets. Those not eaten during the voyage Duke gave to friends back in Newport.

Billy once cooked a whole salmon "Indian style" on the beach of a secluded cove. He nailed the cleaned fish spread open on a board that he leaned against a large rock facing a roaring fire. Heat reflecting off other rocks piled around the fire cooked the fish slowly, leaving it juicy and giving it a delicious smoky taste.

We feasted on the salmon during a picnic on the beach. Duke stood barefoot in the sand, balancing a paper plate heaped with fish and trimmings, and loudly proclaiming—to Billy's vast pleasure—that it was the "best goddamned fish" he'd ever tasted.

BILLY'S HUGE SHIPBOARD FEASTS HELPED DUKE TO PACK ON THE POUNDS BETWEEN PICTURES. *BERNIE ABRAMSON PHOTO*

Wild Goose Flying in the Night Sky

It was no longer true that I was woefully ignorant about John Wayne the film star. Not only did I attend my boss's latest films as they opened in Newport Beach (he was to make twenty-one during my shipboard years), but I was introduced to many of his classic roles from the forties and fifties during screenings at the Bayshore house.

On Friday nights Duke would turn his den into a movie theater for his children and their visiting friends. He owned a 35-mm projector that could show the regular movie-house prints. Perhaps he was grooming me even then as a companion and guardian to his children, but Duke usually asked if I'd like to come over and join them in these screenings. I never hesitated to say yes.

I was amazed on my first visit when Duke pushed a button and a large white screen slowly descended from a false beam in the ceiling. According to the rules of the Screen Actors' Guild, no one—not even Duke—was permitted to operate the 35-mm machine except a licensed projectionist. Duke supported the guild, so he had to hire—at union scale—a professional to come in and run the device.

"We don't do anything halfway around here," he said one night, watching the projectionist thread the film for the start of a show.

Duke also kept a projector aboard the *Goose* for showing 16-mm copies of his and other films. Although he was under no union restrictions when it came to operating a 16-mm projector, he seldom did so. Early on I was designated the official shipboard projectionist for casual screenings held in the main salon or on the afterdeck.

Crew members were always welcome at a showing, provided it didn't interfere with their duties. When the *Goose* was berthed in her Newport slip and the Waynes weren't

SEATTLE FINANCIER MAX WYMAN, THE GOOSE'S PREVIOUS OWNER, RECEIVES A CHRISTMAS PRESENT FROM DUKE ON THE STERN OF WYMAN'S 126-FOOT YACHT, SILVERADO. BERT MINSHALL PHOTO

aboard, the crew would sometimes ask if they could bring their girl-friends aboard to watch a film. It made an impressive—and cheap—date for the lads. Duke didn't mind. "Just keep 'em outta the cabins," he warned.

It was during one of the ship-board screenings that I first saw John Ford's 1959 classic—and one of Duke's personal favorites—*The Searchers*. There's a scene in the film where Duke's co-star, Jeffrey Hunter, unintentionally acquires an Indian woman during a trading session with her tribe. She's a fine, bonny lass, as they say, probably weighing only slightly less than a prairie buffalo. Duke's character, Ethan Edwards, asks the ro-tund woman her name. She replies in dialect that Edwards translates for his companion.

"She says her name is Wild Goose Flying in the Night Sky," he laughs.

The name "Wild Goose" gave me a start. I later asked Ken if Duke had taken the name of the yacht from the movie, but he said it was just coincidence. Apparently, the yacht's former owner, Max Wyman, had bought the boat from a Canadian businessman when she was called *La Beverie*, which Max thought sounded "sissy." He renamed her the *Wild Goose II*—after a dinky, rundown sailboat the ship's cook owned. "It was sort of a joke," explained Ken. But it stuck. All Duke did when he bought the yacht was drop the Roman numeral after the name.

During our first long northern cruise with Duke in 1966, he invited Max Wyman aboard as his guest for a couple of weeks. Although Max would eventually buy what was at the time the world's largest fiberglass-hulled yacht, the 126-foot *Silverado*, he admitted one afternoon that he was a little sorry he'd sold the *Goose*, claiming that he missed "the old girl." I asked him why he'd let her go if he felt that way.

"Aw, hell," said Max, running a hand through his blond hair. "Duke had been aboard a number of times as my guest and fallen in love with her. Said she was big enough to give him some room to move around in. He got it into his head that he wanted to buy her. Mentioned it every time he saw me." Max laughed. "He kept pester-ing me. I could see how much he wanted her, and I really didn't have the time for her then. So I made up my mind, and I told him one day, 'Duke, according to a wise old saying, the two happiest days in a man's life are the day he buys a yacht and the day he sells it. I guess I'm going to make us both happy men.' And I let him have it."

Ken, who had been Max's engineer aboard the *Goose*, agreed to stay aboard and work for Duke. It was an easy choice. Duke was willing to pay him $450 a month—a $50 raise over his current salary. "But Duke didn't know he was giving me a raise," laughed Ken. "Max told me later that when Duke asked him how much I was being paid, he added $50. Duke thought all along he was just matching my current pay." Duke probably would have been tickled that Max had pulled a fast one on him. At any rate, it bloody well tickled Ken.

Duke liked to needle Ken and me about our English heritage. Not long after the yacht's arrival in Newport he purchased an eighteen-foot British Dory to go along with the Boston Whaler. Heavier and with twenty more horsepower than the Whaler

DUKE AT THE WHEEL OF THE
BOSTON WHALER WITH AISSA
AND ETHAN. BEHIND THEM IS THE
NEWLY REMODELED *WILD GOOSE*.
PHIL STERN PHOTO

(although the Whaler had been outfitted with a 115-horsepower motor to give it more muscle for waterskiing), the Dory became Duke's favorite watertaxi. Standing by the sturdy craft he would point a finger and solemnly pronounce:

"The only good thing to ever come out of England is that boat!"

We got our revenge by usually winning the ship's annual World Series baseball betting pool. And we knew next to nothing about the great American pastime. Duke was good-naturedly incredulous. "How the hell did you guys manage that?" he'd mutter as he studied our winning guess, posted on the betting chart in the galley.

Duke enjoyed driving the tenders (especially the Dory), but he wasn't much for in-close maneuvering. He'd bang into the Goose's boarding steps, various docks and pilings with careless abandon. As long as the boat didn't sink, he didn't seem to give a damn what he hit or how often.

Duke liked to tell a story he'd heard about a young navy helmsman trying to bring his motor launch alongside the giant aircraft carrier Enterprise.

"The poor guy made pass after pass, but he just couldn't do it," he explained. "He was getting so frustrated he was actually getting worse instead of better. Well, the captain of the Enterprise was watching this whole episode from the bridge. Finally, he grabs a megaphone and hollers down to the helmsman, 'Hold it right there, Skipper! We'll come alongside of you!' "

That line was a favorite with Duke. Whenever anyone had difficulty maneuvering the Whaler or Dory, he'd lean out over the gunwale and shout it at the struggling pilot. I don't recall, however, anyone ever yelling it at Duke while he was at the controls.

Duke usually joined Pete and me in the wheelhouse as the Goose maneuvered in and out of Newport Bay. It was a half-hour trip at five knots from the yacht's slip to open ocean. Weekend sailors in small sailboats and motor yachts sometimes cut across the Goose's bow in the busy bay, forcing Pete to throw both engines into reverse. I remember once I leaned out from the bridge wingdeck and shouted down at an offending skipper, "Listen, Mate! Do you think we can stop this thing on a dime?"

To the considerable amusement of Duke and Pete, the startled sailor responded with a certain hand signal that told me he didn't care what we could stop on.

On rare occasions Duke took the helm himself. He didn't actually steer a set course. He just pointed the bow where he wanted to go.

Once, as the yacht was approaching her slip, a guest watching in the wheelhouse suggested that Duke take the controls. He refused, well aware that wind and current could make docking tricky for even an experienced skipper.

"We'd probably end up in the parking lot," he said, perhaps with some accuracy.

The Goose was one of the biggest yachts in Newport Harbor. Many times I heard guests happily exclaim as they boarded her for the first time, "This boat's so big I'll never get seasick!" They had an education coming once we made open water.

The Goose's size was deceiving. She'd roll like a harpooned whale in the throes of death in even a moderate sea. Her shallow draft of only nine feet, a relatively narrow twenty-four-foot beam (width), a rounded bottom and an all-wood hull made her extremely buoyant. She'd bob in the swells like a 136-foot-long cork.

Duke never got seasick. Pete and I were similarly blessed. Sometimes we'd be the only ones aboard ship during heavy weather who could manage a meal. As others covered their mouths and sprinted for the side, the three of us would wipe our plates clean and help ourselves to seconds. During one particularly fierce storm in the Sea of Cortez off Baja California, we were forced to sit on the galley deck, our backs braced against a bulkhead so we could steady ourselves long enough to wolf down a hearty breakfast.

Ken, however, could get seasick watching the water swirl away down the bathtub drain. He'd turn green around the gills as the ship rolled in the troughs.

Yet he never complained. He loved the sea and life aboard the *Goose*—at least while we were at anchor or in dock.

Ken once half-jokingly suggested to Duke that he install stabilizers on the yacht. These underwater fins would help keep the ship on a more steady keel. Duke, however, showed no interest in the idea. Ken returned to the engine room, resigned to his fate.

There's an old story about the sailor who returns from a long voyage, sick at heart of the sea, and the first day in port throws an oar across his shoulder and begins walking inland. Puzzled, his shipmates hurry after him and demand an explanation. Without slowing his pace, the retreating sailor points at the oar and shouts back: "The first person I meet who stops me and asks what *this* is, that's where I'm staying!"

When Ken decided to leave the *Goose* in 1973, there were those aboard ship— Duke and me included—who expected him to take up his own symbolic oar and thankfully make for solid ground. Instead, he moved up to Seattle and began a new career—as a commercial fisherman at the helm of his own boat.

Duke had a favorite seasick story about a fellow named Cooley who joined him on his Atlantic crossing on the way to Barcelona.

According to Duke, Cooley owned a big hotel in Bermuda where the yacht had stopped to take on supplies. At a party thrown by the local yachting crowd, Cooley told Duke that he thought crossing the Atlantic aboard a ship like the *Wild Goose* would be the adventure of a lifetime. Duke stopped him with a question.

"You know the one thing standing between you and making that trip?" he asked.

"No, what?"

"A pair of deckshoes!"

Cooley thought he was kidding. But Duke said the offer stood. Cooley weighed this a moment.

"What's ten days out of a lifetime?" he finally decided, accepting the actor's offer.

"That poor sonofabitch," recalled Duke, shaking his head, laughing. "He shows up the next morning with a seabag and excited as a little kid. Says it's the greatest day of his life. Then, before we even make it outta the harbor, he gets sick as a dog. He was hanging over the side losing his breakfast, watching land disappear and looking sorry as hell that he'd come.

"I tried to cheer him up by telling him that he'd probably get his sea legs in a couple days, but that night I'll be damned if we didn't run into gale-force winds. Some of the worst weather I've ever seen. We rolled up to forty-five degrees for a straight fourteen hours.

"Well, Cooley spent most of the time wrapped in a blanket on the afterdeck trying to get some fresh air. He was so miserable he couldn't move. The seas were so huge that the afterdeck was awash. And there moaned ol' Cooley, getting sick all over the deck and just letting the waves comin' through the scuppers wash it overboard. When we finally made the Azores and he set foot on land, he swore that he'd never get back on a boat again." Duke was clearly delighted at the hotel owner's ordeal.

"Ya know," he added, a crooked grin on his face, "if there hadn't been an airport at that place and a plane to take him back home, I bet ol' Cooley would still be there!"

Child's Play Off Catalina

Catalina at first glance was not my idea of an island paradise. Its brown hills looked bone dry. All that water around it, I remember thinking, and apparently not a drop to drink. While Avalon, at Catalina's southeastern tip, was an oasis of palm trees and greenery (a botanical feat made possible by a reservoir built to catch rain runoff), much of the island existed in a rugged and wild state. And yet, there was a stark, even spectacular, beauty to the place. Our voyages to Santa Catalina Island became welcome getaways from the already overdeveloped and crowded mainland.

Catalina had been a great favorite of Duke's for many years. He visited the island often—not only in the *Wild Goose* but in other yachts he'd owned such as the seventy-five-foot *Nor'wester*.

Duke had first fallen in love with Catalina during the 1930s, when he and actor friends such as Ward Bond and Grant Withers visited the island aboard director John Ford's yacht, *Araner*. During one trip, while the *Araner* was moored in the harbor at Avalon, Pappy Ford gave Duke the script of *Stagecoach* to read. Although the great director didn't offer Duke the part of the Ringo Kid—the role that would make him a star—until their return to the mainland, Duke never forgot that trip or the island. His fondness for Santa Catalina ran deep.

Duke and John Ford weren't the island's only Hollywood connection, though. Other stars, including Humphrey Bogart and Errol Flynn, paid regular visits in their own yachts. For decades, dating all the way back to the silent era, movie studios had shot film epics like *Mutiny on the Bounty*, starring Clark Gable, in Catalina waters.

DUKE IN THE LATE 1930S LOOK-ING VERY "HOLLYWOOD NAUTI-CAL" WITH FRIEND BARBARA READ ABOARD THE *VENUS*. *UPI/BETTMANN*

Even the famed Casino ballroom at the entrance to Avalon harbor could boast a little Tinseltown glitz—the art deco murals painted on its walls were by the same artist who painted the murals for Grauman's Chinese Theater in Hollywood.

During my first trip to Catalina, however, I wasn't interested in looking at murals— I was busy scanning the hills for buffalo. On the way over Duke told me about the herd of wild bison that roamed the island. I was excited. Even a Liverpool lad knew about buffalo. They were big and shaggy and for some reason they always stampeded over hapless settlers in Western movies. For an hour I peered through a pair of binoculars without seeing so much as a hoof. I finally gave up. Although I would catch glimpses of the legendary beasts grazing in the Catalina hills many times over the years—I even saw a herd once strolling along a beach—all I saw that first trip were goats.

I was making about three hundred dollars a month in those days, not much even then; but by living aboard ship and having meals and uniforms provided free, I'd saved enough to buy a four-hundred-horsepower speedboat. On the *Goose*'s next trip to Catalina, I persuaded Pete Stein to let me tow the sleek craft behind the yacht for a trial run at the island.

We anchored off White's Cove, about four or five miles up the coast from Avalon. The calm water here was excellent for waterskiing, there was a fine white sand beach, and there were coastal reefs for fishing and good hiking trails in the nearby hills. Although Duke would sometimes order us to Avalon, or north to the island's isthmus at Two Harbors, White's was by far his favorite Catalina destination.

This afternoon Duke was curious about my high-octane toy. As I revved the boat's motor he leaned over the stern taffrail. The roar was deafening. I loved it. I

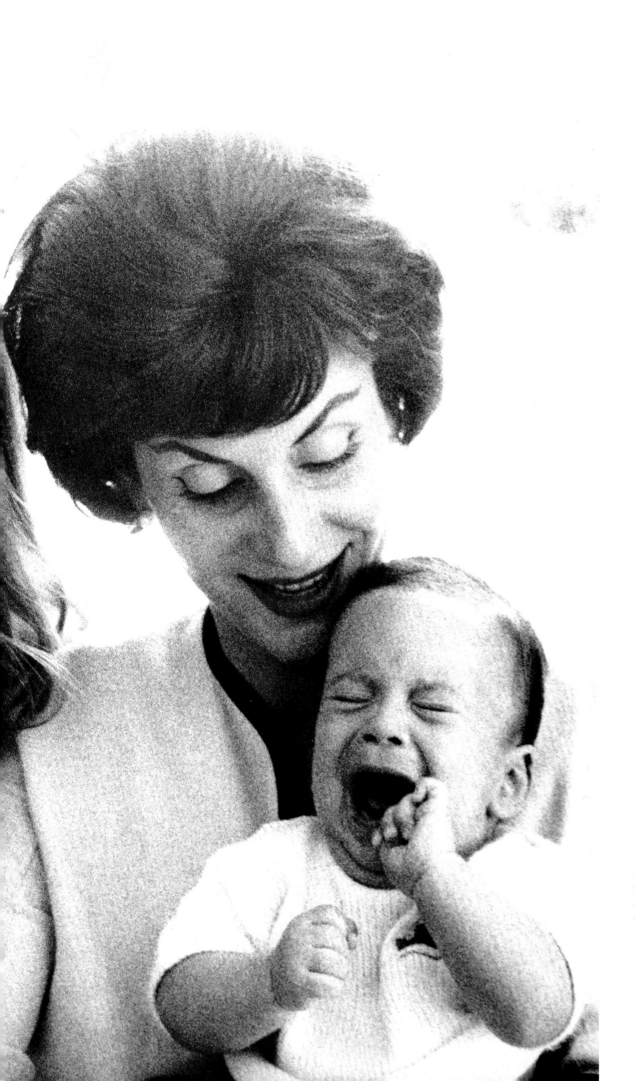

DUKE GETS A SECOND SHOT AT FATHERHOOD DOTING ON AISSA AND ETHAN. *BERNIE ABRAMSON PHOTO*

noticed Duke watching, and, without really thinking about it, asked if he'd like to go for a spin around the cove.

"You sure that thing is safe?" he asked, eyeing the coughing and rumbling muscle-boat. I told him I thought so (although I wasn't really sure myself). Duke was game. "Okay," he decided. "Let's see what she'll do."

With Duke settled into the seat beside me, I drove several yards from the *Goose*, then hit the throttle. Hard. We shot forward, picking up speed so fast that the G-force slammed us back in our seats. The acceleration was extraordinary. We were doing close to seventy miles per hour as we shot across the cove, the hull thudding and banging as we "porpoised" over the swells. I eased back on the gas and brought the boat into a sliding turn.

The return run was even faster. The boat roared over the water, the bow dipping low as we raced toward the *Goose*. Duke, bouncing up and down beside me, looked straight ahead, saying nothing, as he had the entire run. I pulled back on the throttle and the boat quickly slowed, a berm of water spreading out before it. We drifted the last dozen yards to the yacht.

I was excited from the ride and asked Duke how he'd liked it. He ran a big hand over his bald head and turned in his seat.

"Between you and me," he said evenly, "I like the Boston Whaler better."

•

DUKE ONCE CALLED CATALINA HIS HAVEN AWAY FROM THE "BUSTLE AND BULLSHIT" OF the mainland. It was a typical turn of phrase for a man whose verbal fireworks could blister the paint on a bulkhead.

Yet, for the most part, it was an easy sort of profanity Duke practiced. More habit than anything else, really, picked up from years spent around tough-talking film crews. I never heard him try to savage another person by using an obscenity. As the saying goes, he pretty much swore for the hell of it.

(I understand that Duke's secretary of twenty-five years, Mary St. John, would routinely sanitize her boss's language in business letters. Duke would be cussing and swearing as he dictated to Mary, who would then type a finished letter whose prose was clean enough to read in Sunday School.)

He tried to clean up his language around his children—which could be difficult in the close quarters aboard ship. One afternoon after a quick trip into Avalon in the Boston Whaler, Duke forgot to duck as he climbed the boarding ladder and struck his head against an overhang on the sidedeck.

"SHIT!" he exploded, just as Ethan, age five, bounded through the main salon's open door. Seeing the boy, he quickly tried to cover himself.

"Oh . . . ah, I mean shoot," Duke stammered.

Duke's linguistic concern was possibly prompted by an incident that had taken place aboard ship a few days before. Ethan was trying to reach Billy Sweatt down in the galley using the ship's intercom in his parent's stateroom. But there was no response. I was passing by the galley when I heard a young voice rattling the intercom speaker.

"Billy! Billy! Billy! For Chrissakes! Isn't there anyone in that damn galley?"

There was little mystery where the boy had picked up such spirited language. Like father, like son.

One afternoon while watching Ethan scamper around the *Goose*'s toy-strewn after-

WITH AISSA AND A POUTY ETHAN ABOARD THE BOSTON WHALER. GLOBE PHOTOS

deck, Duke was reminded of an experiment he'd read about, illustrating the vast energy of young children.

"This Marine Corps sergeant was supposed to follow this little five-year-old kid around and mimic exactly every move he made during the course of a normal day," recalled Duke. "By evening that Marine—a really tough guy in top physical shape—was exhausted, but the kid was still goin' strong!"

We both could sympathize with that Marine. The Wayne children, especially Ethan, were like pint-sized cyclones.

Limited by the loss of a lung, Duke realized that he could no longer romp and play with his youngsters as much as he would have liked. Whether it was through coincidence or design, I assumed the role of active playmate, as well as guardian and confidant to his kids.

It wasn't long before I was spending most of my shipboard hours with the children. I had as much fun as they did during our happy days together waterskiing, swimming and just plain goofing off. Although Pete wryly dubbed me "head of the diaper detail," he realized how important it was that someone always keep an eye on the youngsters, especially aboard ship. It just irked him that I enjoyed it so much.

Ken failed to share my easy camaraderie with the spirited Wayne offspring. He lacked my patience with the youngsters. I suppose I was something of a pushover. The children knew they could twist me around their little fingers. But not Ken.

Ken was the disciplinarian aboard ship. He tolerated no nonsense. This could lead to confrontations, such as the time off Two Harbors when Ken reprimanded Ethan on the afterdeck for some now forgotten reason. The boy was furious. He turned and shouted, "I hate you!" Then, in a reckless move, he spit on the nearest available target—Ken's kneecap.

I figured Ethan was headed for a spanking, but Ken, adopting the Biblical notion of "an eye for an eye," retaliated by spitting on the boy's head. I'm not certain what Dr. Benjamin Spock, the guru of child-raising, would have said about this sort of child-adult exchange, but it had the desired effect—the boy was so shocked that he never spit at Ken—or anyone else—again.

I sometimes think Ethan liked to test the adults around him. I was patient with the boy, but I wasn't a saint. Once while I was coiling the ski line in the stern of the Whaler I warned Ethan not to touch the throttle. Of course, as soon as I turned my back, that's precisely what he did. The boat lurched forward, and I nearly catapulted over the outboard motor. I was furious. Without thinking I grabbed Ethan by the throat with both hands and screamed, "Why, you little sonofabitch!" Even in my anger, though, I realized that this was no way to behave with the boy. I let go. I expected Ethan to be thoroughly cowed by my display, but instead, he seemed absolutely delighted. "Do that again!" he laughed. I guess he was thrilled that he'd got such a rise out of me.

Yet for all Ethan's mischievous ways, he remained at heart a very affectionate boy. We became the best of pals. One afternoon Pilar returned in the Whaler from a shopping trip into Avalon and presented us with matching black-and-white T-shirts (black and white were Pilar's favorite colors). Ethan loved to wear that T-shirt, but only if I would wear mine at the same time.

In the spring of 1966 a curious and touching episode took place on the beach at White's. It was late afternoon, and Ethan and I were playing tag in the sand.

Suddenly, Ethan stopped running. I walked over to see what was the matter. Before I could say anything, he reached up and grabbed my hand.

"Do you mind if I call you Dad?" he asked, staring up at me. I didn't know what to say. I looked at the boy, wondering how to handle this.

"Gee, Ethan, that would really hurt your dad's feelings."

He thought it over a moment.

"Well," he said, still holding my hand. "Then just for today."

I later realized that this was the sort of innocent request an impressionable young boy might make. He probably failed to understand fully why his father could not do all the things with him that I could.

Duke had long regretted not spending more time with his children from his first marriage. He felt he'd neglected Michael, Patrick, Toni and Melinda because he was

LEFT: BERT SHARES A HAPPY SHIP-BOARD MOMENT WITH ETHAN OFF CATALINA.

UPPER RIGHT: A SUNNY DAY ON THE HICKEA. BERT MINSHALL PHO-TOS (2)

too busy making movies. Now that he had a second family and a chance to make up for past mistakes, he often wasn't physically up to joining the children in their more vigorous activities. That duty usually fell to me, which meant that my day-to-day contact with the children was often greater than their own father's. It was an irony that I'm sure didn't escape Duke.

Although flattered that Ethan would want to call me "Dad," I hoped it was a passing fancy. When we returned to the ship later that afternoon I was apprehensive. But when Ethan saw his father on the afterdeck, he ran to him and threw his arms around his neck. Duke kissed his son and lifted him in his arms. I had mixed feelings watching them but was overall very much relieved.

Almost ten years would pass before I told Duke about that afternoon at White's. I was riding in the rear seat of a rental car as the actor drove with his secretary, Pat Stacy (Mary St. John had recently retired), to the airport outside of Puerto Vallarta, Mexico. Duke had spent several weeks cruising aboard the yacht and was now flying back to Newport.

We were discussing the recent events of the voyage when the conversation turned to children—Duke's in particular—and the funny things they often do and say when very young. I don't know why, but I told him what Ethan had said to me at Catalina so many years before. I suppose I thought he would get a kick out of it. Perhaps I also wanted to pump up my own ego. When I finished he half turned in his seat and looked at me over his shoulder.

"The hell he did?" he said, obviously surprised. He turned back to watch the road. We drove on to the airport, Pat trying to make small talk by commenting on the passing scenery, asking Duke questions and listening brightly to his replies. But somehow the conversation never got back on track.

•

I PUT THE CARPENTRY SKILLS I ACQUIRED AROUND THE DOCKS AND WHARFS OF MERSEYSIDE to good use as chief builder of toy boats for the children. The kids would gather in the carpentry shop I set up in the old bo'sun's locker forward of the galley to supervise the construction of vessels from scrap blocks of wood. I was kept busy because they were forever losing them over the side or setting them adrift.

One day Ethan entered the bo'sun's locker as I was doing some varnishing. He asked if I would build him another toy boat. I asked him what happened to the first half-dozen or so I'd made for him. "They sank," he explained. I told him I doubted that, noting the buoyant properties of wood, but agreed to construct another vessel.

Unknown to me, Duke was sitting in the galley with the skipper as I set to work. As soon as he heard the sound of my saw biting into wood he let out a roar.

"My God!" he exclaimed in mock horror. "What's that Bert doin' now?"

It became something of a joke with Duke that I seemed to be always sawing or sanding on the yacht. He claimed that I would eventually turn the ship into a 287-ton pile of sawdust.

It frightened Pilar when she couldn't find the children in their usual play areas aboard ship. She'd be terrified they had fallen overboard. But she soon learned to check the bo'sun's locker before alarming the crew. More times than not, Aissa, Ethan and Marisa would be there, happily huddled around my workbench as I crafted yet another vessel for their toy fleets.

DUKE AND THREE OF HIS FOUR OLDER CHILDREN ABOARD THE *NOR'WESTER* OFF CATALINA DURING THE 1950S. PATRICK (TOP), TONI (CENTER, RIGHT), AND MELINDA (LOWER). FLIP STERN (CENTER), THE YOUNG BOY LOOKING UP AT DUKE, IS THE SON OF THE PHOTOGRAPHER. *PHIL STERN PHOTO*

I did my best to avoid favoritism among the children. But by the time I took an active role in their lives, ten-year-old Aissa was already finding friends and interests away from the *Wild Goose*. I ended up spending far more time with Ethan and Marisa than with Duke's older girl. As a result, she would never grant me the same blind devotion that her younger brother and sister did.

Yet as she matured, so did our friendship. I suppose I played more the part of big brother, giving advice when it was welcome, learning to shut my mouth when it was not.

I believe a side of Duke secretly mourned the maturing of Aissa into a young woman. He used to play with her by the hour when she was a little girl, throwing her up in the air, smothering her with affection. Aissa, in turn, idolized her father. As she grew older, though, I think Duke's love became a little overwhelming for her. Her father was like a force of nature. The love ran deep between them, but sometimes Aissa had to hold onto herself to keep from being blown away.

As for me, it was important that I strike a balance between being the children's companion and their protector. Especially in the case of Marisa. Just as he'd been with Aissa, Duke was extremely protective of his youngest daughter. Sometimes I wasn't sure when to stop being a play pal and start being a watchdog. Duke would usually let me know—loudly—when I made the wrong choice. And, yet, he could be unexpectedly

encouraging of Marisa's adventurous spirit.

When Marisa was about seven, she asked me if she could dive from the roof of the master stateroom. Diving and jumping from the *Goose*'s upper decks were favorite pastimes of the more daring aboard ship. That afternoon she'd been watching Ethan and me take turns plunging into the cool water off White's. As she was wont to do at this time, she was determined to keep up with "the boys."

Although Marisa had jumped feet first from that height, she'd never attempted a dive. I was uneasy about letting her try. I took the coward's way out and told her she'd better ask her dad for permission first. She scampered off to the boatdeck. A moment later Duke shouted at me, "Go ahead and let her do it."

The twenty-five feet from the roof to the water probably seemed like a hundred to Marisa. She hesitated, her toes curled down over the roof's edge. She was having a serious case of pre-dive jitters.

Then I heard Duke shouting from the boatdeck.

"C'mon, Marisa! You can do it!" he bellowed, exhorting her on. Ethan and I, waiting in the water below, joined in. Finally, Marisa clasped her hands over her head like a Hindu dancer, gathered in a deep breath, and pushed off. She dropped in a pretty arc, entering the water with a small splash. It was a surprisingly clean dive. I looked up at Duke. He was smiling, every inch the proud papa.

"Well done, Marisa!" he shouted, clapping his hands. "Well done!"

Left: With Aissa, age seven, in the *Goose*'s wheelhouse. The original navy radar (right) was later donated to the Sea Scouts in Newport Beach. *Black Star photo*

Upper Right: With three-year-old Ethan. *Globe Photos*

Right: An acrobatic Marisa on the taffrail. *Bert Minshall photo*

At Home in Newport

Duke's ties to Newport Beach went back almost forty years, to the 1920s, when he was a freshman at the University of Southern California. He was Marion Michael Morrison then, a star on the USC football team and a devotee of bodysurfing during the summers off the beaches of Newport's Balboa peninsula. According to Duke, it was bodysurfing that ended his football career, when he tore the muscles in one shoulder.

But if the Newport surf cost him a spot on the gridiron—as well as his football scholarship—it indirectly gave him his start in films. He was forced to leave school to take a job—as a grip manhandling props at a movie studio. In a way, a rogue wave set Duke on the path to stardom.

Duke would sometimes reminisce as the *Goose* made her way through Newport Harbor about the times he and his Sigma Chi fraternity buddies would drive down from Los Angeles for long weekends at the Orange County resort. There were a lot of memories here. He met his first wife, Josephine Saenz (mother of his four older children), at the old Balboa Inn. He'd gone to dances at the Balboa Pavilion, built in 1905 and still a landmark on the bay. There were long afternoons spent sliding on the bay's mud flats (now long gone), followed by a sprint across the narrow Balboa peninsula to wash off with a swim in the cool Pacific. And, as local legend tells it, he brawled his way through more than one saloon during a night of high-spirited drinking.

"Yeah, I guess I did my share of fightin'," he laughed years later when I finally asked him if the stories of his brawling were true. "But I never started it. I was just defending myself. Of course, I defended myself a *lot* in those days." Duke explained how he'd once fought a fellow who bet fifty dollars he could whip him. I asked what happened. A crooked grin crossed his face.

"I let him keep the fifty to pay for some new teeth!"

Duke wasn't the only film star drawn to Newport Beach. Song-and-dance man (and Davy Crockett's sidekick on the original *Disneyland* TV show) Buddy Ebsen, cowboy stars Roy Rogers and Dale Evans, director-leading man Dick Powell and good friends Andy Devine and Claire Trevor (Duke's co-stars in *Stagecoach)*, all had homes around the bay at one time. Bogart and Errol Flynn once moored their yachts there. But there was little doubt that Duke was the most sought out—and accessible—of the Newport Beach movie colony.

Harbor tour boats, passing yachters, kids on paddle boards, all hove to as they sailed by the Bayshore house or the *Goose*'s berth at Lido Yacht Anchorage, hoping to get a glimpse of John Wayne. If they spotted him, there would be cameras clicking and voices bellowing, "Howdy, Duke!" Duke always smiled and waved back, gracious in the face of the continual invasions of his privacy.

Duke unquestionably enjoyed getting out and meeting people, although he disliked

mob scenes. He'd run to the local stores to pick up items for the house or boat. Over the years I've met a number of people who claim to have run into Duke in this way. I have no reason to doubt them. Sometimes the run-ins were almost literal, such as the time the former girlfriend of a buddy of mine unknowingly stepped into Duke's path as he strode down the aisle of a Newport Beach drug store. "Well, howdy, little lady," he drawled, gazing down at her. He left her wide-eyed as he headed for the checkout register.

Duke had a secret for getting through crowds of fans quickly by handing out cards printed with his signature and the salutation, "GOOD LUCK." On trips ashore I'd carry an extra supply of these cards. Sometimes the crowds were so big Duke would run out, and he'd send me back to the *Goose* for more. As a joke he once had replicas of Confederate money printed with his picture on the back. I don't know if he ever handed any out, though, except to friends.

Duke considered the *Goose* his sanctuary away from the maddening crowd. He'd smile and wave to people on shore or aboard other yachts, but he seldom struck up conversations. When people complimented him on the *Goose*, he would invariably respond, "Yeah, she's a honey, isn't she?" At least once, though, Duke mused about how he wished the navy had not removed the old minesweeper's 50-mm bowgun (whose iron supports could still be seen in a compartment below the foredeck). He joked that he could have used it to fire a warning shot or two over the heads of pushy fans.

Sometimes the owners of other large yachts would invite Duke aboard their boats. Usually—unless, of course, the owner was a friend—he'd politely decline, although once up in British Columbia he responded to an invitation by shouting out, "You come over and see *my* yacht!" The startled—and thrilled—yacht owners did just that, as Duke proudly showed them around the *Goose*.

All in all, Duke genuinely appreciated the loyalty of his fans and was deeply moved by their heartfelt displays of affection, especially in later years, as his health began to

THE BREAKFAST NOOK OFF THE
LIVING ROOM. PILAR FEEDS
MARISA AS AISSA LOOKS ON. TO
THE LEFT OF DUKE AND ETHAN IS
PART OF THE BLACK LAVA-ROCK
FIREPLACE DESIGNED BY PILAR.
JOHN DOMINIS/LIFE MAGAZINE

fail. While other celebrities might hide behind squads of bodyguards or glide by in their anonymous limousines on the way to some exclusive boutique, Duke could often be found standing in the sunlight on his bayfront patio waving to well-wishers, or making small talk with a fan he'd met in a local market.

•

DUKE'S BAYSHORE HOME WAS SPACIOUS AND COMFORTABLE, IF A LITTLE ON THE cluttered side. It was decorated with an odd combination of Oriental and Western art—sort of Far East meets the Wild West. Dominating the living room was an enormous fireplace built entirely of black lava rock, which Duke told me Pilar had designed.

Duke believed in his comfort. In the master bedroom he installed a television in the ceiling. It descended at the push of a button so he and Pilar could watch in bed.

The heart of the home, though, was Duke's large, wood-paneled study—an exact copy of the study in his Encino ranch home. Awards and mementos Duke had picked up over the years crowded display areas built into the walls. His extensive collection of Hopi Indian Kachina dolls, brilliantly painted and decorated with beads and feathers, stood on an overhead shelf that ran the length of the room.

I think, though, that more than anything, I was impressed by the stacks of books and magazines everywhere. Duke was an avid reader whose interests included history, biography, philosophy and current fiction. He was a great fan of Winston Churchill's writings. This is a side of Duke the public seldom, if ever, saw. It's easy to forget that he attended college at a time when most people simply graduated from high school and went straight to work. He was a scholar in high school—a straight-A student, class president and member of the debate team. He even managed to win a Shakespearean oratory contest! As he was fond of saying, he had to learn to say "ain't" for the movies because "they didn't teach it at USC."

AN EXUBERANT DUKE AND PILAR ON A COOL FALL DAY OUTSIDE THEIR NEWPORT BEACH HOME. *PHIL STERN PHOTO*

Duke's screen image portrayed him as a tough action hero. Yet during my years aboard the *Wild Goose*, I also saw a refined man who played chess, sipped Napoleon brandy and appreciated a good book.

Duke was a man of manners—unless he was behind the wheel of his green Pontiac station wagon. Then it was every man, woman and pedestrian for themselves.

A drive with Duke was an experience to remember—if not dread. He drove as if he had blinders on. Rearview mirrors, in his opinion, were for sissies. I got the impression he drove from place to place the way some men shave in the morning—unaware that he had a potentially deadly weapon in hand. Yet he never, to my knowledge, had an accident or received a traffic citation. I don't know how he avoided the first, but as far as the second is concerned, I believe that as long as Duke's Pontiac was on the right side of the road and had not obviously run over any old ladies crossing the street, the local police tended to look the other way as he went by. Stardom has its perks.

The Pontiac was well known around Newport Beach because of its distinctive bubble top. Duke had had the roof raised seven inches by Barris of Hollywood, the self-proclaimed "King of the Customizers," so that he could wear his Stetson hat while driving. He complained that most cars were too small and cramped. "They're built for women," he'd complain. "A man needs more room to stretch out in."

The garage at the Bayshore house was usually so crammed with bicycles, old toys, broken appliances and miscellaneous junk that there was little room left for the station wagon. Duke had a lot in common with most people on this count. Later, as Ethan grew older, a couple of motorcycles and a dune buggy were added to the crush. Duke usually ended up keeping the Pontiac parked in the driveway.

Duke didn't always drive himself. For longer trips he would have his personal "gofer," Barney Farthingham, take over the driving chores. But around town, Duke was often the man in the driver's seat.

Local residents always knew when Duke was visiting a certain store or restaurant in Newport Beach or nearby Costa Mesa. All they had to do was look in the parking lot for the big green Pontiac station wagon with the raised roof and the bumper sticker that read, "The Marines Are Looking For A Few Good Men."

•

AT ONE TIME DUKE KEPT FOUR DOGS AT THE BAYSHORE HOUSE. TWO MINIATURE Doberman pinschers and two unclassified mutts. Duke said the whole bunch couldn't corner a rat if each was armed with a Colt .45.

I used to fight my way through this tail-wagging, slobbering, panting, jumping welcoming committee every time I used the yard gate at the back of the house. The children loved the dogs. The gardeners hated them. Chewed newspapers often littered the yard. Bushes and flowers were dug up. Not to mention the toxic waste that four dogs on one lawn could leave behind.

"Christ," Duke would swear as he picked a careful path through the grass. "Watch your step. I've seen horses that crap less than those dogs."

Duke actually preferred a more natural look to the grounds and flowerbeds of his estate, although at times the dogs made it a little too natural. One afternoon I came across him wistfully gazing over a hedge into the perfectly groomed yard of his next-door neighbor.

"Makes mine look like a goddamn jungle," he muttered.

Up North

Duke was awed by the scenic magnitude of the Pacific Northwest and its fabled Inside Passage. Stretching from Seattle, Washington, up coastal British Columbia to Glacier Bay, Alaska, this thousand-mile expanse of pristine inlets and lakes is a popular summer sailing ground. Formed by the receding glaciers of the Ice Age, it had a secluded beauty (and great salmon fishing) that would draw Duke on trips aboard the *Wild Goose* again and again over the years.

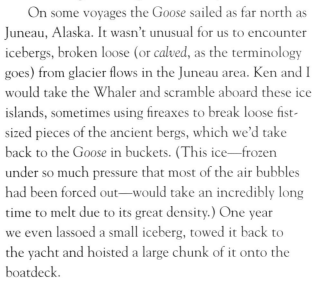

MARISA AND HER FATHER WITH A THIRTY-POUND SALMON, CAUGHT IN BIG BAY, STUART ISLAND. *BERT MINSHALL PHOTO*

On some voyages the *Goose* sailed as far north as Juneau, Alaska. It wasn't unusual for us to encounter icebergs, broken loose (or *calved*, as the terminology goes) from glacier flows in the Juneau area. Ken and I would take the Whaler and scramble aboard these ice islands, sometimes using fireaxes to break loose fist-sized pieces of the ancient bergs, which we'd take back to the *Goose* in buckets. (This ice—frozen under so much pressure that most of the air bubbles had been forced out—would take an incredibly long time to melt due to its great density.) One year we even lassoed a small iceberg, towed it back to the yacht and hoisted a large chunk of it onto the boatdeck.

Duke was fascinated by the glacier flows but usually preferred exploring warmer climes such as the Sunshine Coast and Discovery Passage areas of lower British Columbia—in particular, Princess Louisa Inlet, about seventy miles north of Vancouver. Like White's Cove at Catalina and Mazatlán on the Mexican coast, Princess Louisa (named in honor of the mother of Queen Victoria) became one of Duke's favorite cruising spots. Its heroic sweep of cliffs and mountains—some towering eight thousand feet above the inlet—has earned Princess Louisa the nickname "Yosemite of the North."

The prize jewel in the Princess Louisa scenic crown is Chatterbox Falls, a 120-foot-high cataract that thunders down a heavily wooded cliff into the inlet's calm water. Duke, who liked to view the falls from the *Goose*'s bow, would urge Pete Stein to nose the yacht as close to the torrent as he dared. Many times the wind-driven spray would whip across the foredeck, soaking Duke and his guests.

Invariably, Duke would organize an expedition to go ashore for a climb to the top of Chatterbox. From numerous ledges it's possible—though not advisable—to stick a hand into the falls themselves. As many as a dozen people (no one really knows for sure) have slipped on the wet, moss-covered rocks and plummeted into the violent cascade. We all had a bad scare during one visit in the early seventies when Ethan, walking near the waterfall's edge, lost his balance and slid several feet, landing heavily on his hands and knees on the slippery rocks. Another yard and he would have gone over the side to almost certain death.

To help ward off the chilly nights during our annual cruises north, I'd bring with me a heavy wool sweater that my mother had given me back in England. The tag sewn in its collar claimed it had been handcrafted by a "genuine North American Indian." Duke greatly admired it, exclaiming at least once a trip, "Damn, that's a good lookin' sweater!" I would have given it to him, but we were about seventy pounds apart from being able to share the same wardrobe.

RIGHT AND BELOW: NORTH TO ALASKA *BERT MINSHALL PHOTOS*

If Duke enjoyed the scenery of British Columbia, he was a fanatic for the salmon fishing. He'd fish every day for weeks sometimes, roaring away at dawn with the local fishing guides, returning for a quick lunch and then going out again until supper and, when the fever was really upon him, out once more until it got dark—which up north meant around 10 p.m. He'd bring back salmon that were bigger than Marisa. Sometimes he'd take his children with him for a morning or afternoon's fishing. It always delighted him when they managed to catch a bigger salmon than he did.

About a hundred miles north of Vancouver is a fisherman's nirvana called Big Bay, Stuart Island. Here Duke embarked on his salmon marathons, accompanied by a local fishing guide named John Davies. One year over a three-week period Duke spent close to four thousand dollars with the guide—which always made the *Goose* a welcome sight as she pulled into the bay to begin her annual visits. Without fail Mrs. Davies would greet us dockside on our arrival with a big basket of homemade bread. As Duke hugged the happy woman with one arm, he'd devour slice after buttered slice cut from the still-warm loaves.

•

ON AN EARLY TRIP NORTH MAX WYMAN presented Duke with a small brass cannon for the *Wild Goose*. It was an instant hit with the children, as well as with Duke and the crew.

Duke recruited Ken as the yacht's official artillery officer. Working with ramrod, black powder and paper wadding, Ken quickly grew expert at producing a

LEFT: ICEBERGS WERE A COMMON SIGHT WHEN CRUISING IN ALASKAN WATERS. BERT AND CREWMAN BREAK OFF ICY CHUNKS TO TAKE BACK TO THE GOOSE, WHILE KEN MINSHALL (LOWER LEFT) TAKES A RIDE ON A DRIFTING ISLAND OF ICE.

LOWER RIGHT: IN TRACEY ARM NEAR JUNEAU, ALASKA. BERT MINSHALL PHOTOS (3)

deafening—though otherwise harmless—bang. I'm just glad he didn't detonate himself while priming and loading the piece.

It was a runt of a cannon, about two feet long, but it sure got the job done. Stand too close as it thundered a salute and your ears would ring for ten minutes from the concussion. The ratio of cannon to boom was out of all proportion. It was as if a small lizard had suddenly reared up on its hind legs and roared like Godzilla.

The first time we fired it Duke was standing a few feet behind Ken, watching as my fearless brother touched a lighted match to a fuse in the priming hole. The fuse sizzled a moment. Then there followed a great flash and what sounded like a thunderclap going off inside a phone booth. An acrid-smelling cloud of white smoke hung in the air.

"Packs a wallop, don't she," drawled Duke, looking pleased.

Whenever we fired the cannon, the smell of burnt powder reminded me of my childhood in England during the blitz of the Second World War. I thought of the pungent, unforgettable odor of exploded bombs hanging in the air for days following a German air attack. Ken and I made a game of wandering through shell craters and the rubble of buildings collecting bomb fragments for souvenirs. All our friends did it, trading the twisted pieces of metal at school like prize marbles.

Duke liked to drag the cannon out from time to time for the firing of salutes or the booming entertainment of the children. The Fourth of July was a big day for the gun. Ken's hands would turn

black from handling the powder as he loaded charge after charge into the breech. Actually, using the cannon to celebrate the noisy American holiday turned out to be much safer than the time we set off fireworks and scorched the point on the boatdeck.

We seemed to use the cannon more while cruising the inlets of the Pacific Northwest than anywhere else. We'd exchange smoky salutes with cannons belonging to inhabitants who lived along the isolated waterways.

I remember when actor and good friend Hugh O'Brien joined Duke for a week's cruising. We went ashore at one spot to pick blueberries (Duke loved Billy's fresh blueberry pie) and met an old fellow who had mounted an ancient brass field piece on a pine stump near his log cabin.

This grizzled gentleman was exceedingly proud of that cannon—nearly as much as he was of the fact that he'd been born with an extra finger on each hand, as well as a bonus toe on each foot (his parents had had the excess fingers surgically removed when he was a child—an act for which he'd never quite forgiven them). Duke and Hugh inspected the beat-up artillery piece. It looked as if it had been on the losing side at Waterloo. In a neighborly gesture, our host offered to fire the old gun off. Duke hesitated.

"Aw, hell, that's okay," he finally said, eyeing the tarnished and dented relic—the cannon, that is—with distrust. But the ancient cannoneer was itching to let loose a blast. I had already decided that if it came to that, I wasn't going to stick around for the fun. Duke and Hugh were apparently of a like mind. Duke clapped a hand on the old man's shoulder.

"Sorry, friend, but we just don't have the time," he told him. The old man's face fell like a punctured English pudding. Duke cheered him up, however, by suggesting that he fire a round when we got back to the *Wild Goose*, anchored in the cove below. "That way it'd be sort of a send-off salute," he suggested. Our host lit up at the

idea. He shook hands all around and watched happily as we hiked down the hill.

As Duke climbed aboard the British Dory at the water's edge, however, he shook his head.

"I sure hope he doesn't blow himself to kingdom come with that thing."

From the *Goose's* afterdeck we could just make out the cabin through the pines. All was calm when a puff of smoke billowed from the trees. Then we heard the boom of cannon fire. It was an anxious moment before a figure emerged from the woods and waved. It was our friend, alive and apparently with all his remaining fingers intact. Duke laughed and asked Ken to fire our own cannon in response.

While passing through Malibu Rapids, at the entrance to Princess Louisa Inlet, we'd traditionally exchange cannon salutes with a youth camp located there. Boys and girls would swarm over a rocky outcropping and excitedly shout for Duke to come out on deck. He always obliged. As the yacht drew abreast of the waving youngsters, the smoky duel would begin.

"Let 'er rip!" Duke would bellow as Ken lit the cannon's primer, sending a fiery cloud of smoke and burnt paper out through an open hatchway in the gunwale. A moment later, the camp's cannon would return the broadside. As long as the camp remained in sight, Ken continued loading and firing. Smoke from the barrage soon hung in low drifting clouds over the water. The boys and girls loved the roaring exchange, as did the Wayne children. Those somewhat older children in the crew also had a grand time. And through it all, as he watched from the afterdeck, Duke would be grinning like John Paul Jones about to send another British man-o'-war to the bottom.

ANCHORED OFF CHATTERBOX FALLS IN PRINCESS LOUISA INLET, BRITISH COLUMBIA. *BERT MINSHALL PHOTO*

Spit, Drink and Be Merry

After losing a lung to cancer, Duke underwent one long, agonizing nicotine fit. He missed cigarettes, and for months after his operation he'd let anyone within earshot know it.

"Damn!" he'd swear. "But I'm dyin' for a smoke."

To help satisfy his craving for cigarettes he switched to chewing tobacco. Red Man and Beechnut were his favorite brands. Pilar gamely went along with her husband's newest vice. Just so he didn't start smoking again.

Duke could be a dangerous man with a load of tobacco juice in his mouth. His aim was true but his targets were random. He was a special hazard aboard ship. One day, while under way for Catalina, he and his actor son, Patrick Wayne, were talking on the bow. Both were working large wads of tobacco and spitting into the sea. I was in the wheelhouse when a brown spray whipped across the windows. Duke had launched a liquid boomerang, the wind catching the juice and flinging it back across the foredeck. It taught me never to stand downwind of him on the high seas.

I wasn't an eyewitness to this, but I once met a woman who claimed she'd had a close call one afternoon when Duke nearly spit on her in the parking lot of a local store. Apparently, the woman had spotted him leaving the store and was hurrying to catch up so she could get an autograph when he turned his head and let go with a stream of brown liquid. It hit at her feet, stopping her in her tracks. Duke never even

DUKE WITH PATRICK. FATHER AND SON OFTEN SHARED A CHAW OF TOBACCO WHILE ABOARD. *PHIL STERN PHOTO*

saw her. He kept right on walking, getting into his station wagon and driving away, oblivious that he'd come close to bagging a fan.

One of Pete Stein's more gruesome misadventures took place following a chewing session by Duke and Patrick on the after- deck. Father and son had been spitting into a Styrofoam cup, gradually filling it about halfway with dark liquid. They left it on the poker table when they were through.

Pete was always leaving coffee cups around ship. He had a habit of finishing off their contents as he came across them. That's because they were usually spiked with J&B scotch. Pete was not a man to waste whisky needlessly. This must have been on his mind when he found that dangerous cup on the afterdeck. I won't go into details, but I was just in time to see the look of horror on his face when he realized he'd been poisoned. He nearly ran over me in a mad sprint for the crew's head. From that day forth Pete cast a wary eye on any stray cup until he'd verified it was not a booby trap.

Duke was a man of strong habit. Especially when the habit came in a tobacco pouch or could be poured out of a bottle. One afternoon I drove over to the Newport house to discuss some ship's business. When five o'clock hit—cocktail hour—Duke offered me a tequila on the rocks.

"I think you'll like this," he said, walking over to a small portable bar set up on one side of the room. He dropped some ice cubes into two large glasses and filled them to the brim from a bottle of Sauza Commerativo—his favorite brand—then shoved a glass in my hand.

One sip and I almost gagged. Never much of a booze hound, I used to cut my beer with Seven-Up, called a *shandy* in England (although in recent years I've grown rather fond of rum and Coke). This was out of my league. But I told Duke it was great. So smooth and tasty. I didn't have the guts to tell him I thought it tasted like a solution used to pickle tarantulas.

But Duke loved tequila. Aboard ship he could finish off an entire bottle during the course of a day. But no matter the consumption, I never saw him drunk—just happy as hell.

Duke was a powerful and a steady drinker. Others around him might dissolve into alcohol-soaked puddles, but Duke always remained on his feet, coherent and coordi- nated. I suppose he was the classic example of a two-fisted drinker. He simply possessed a physical capacity for booze that few others could match.

"I've always had a lot of fun drinking," he once said. "I'm Irish, ya know, and the Irish are a *very* thirsty race."

I don't recall when Duke switched from brandy to tequila as his preferred drink. In his younger days I understand he was a bourbon man.

Considering all the time Duke spent aboard the *Wild Goose* cruising in southern

waters, the change to tequila was not surprising. I once met a fellow who claimed he
was the first person to introduce Duke to the Mexican national liquor. In fact, I've
known several chaps who claim exactly the same thing. Wherever and however he discovered the fiery booze, Duke was its dedicated consumer.

Pilar seldom drank aboard ship. She often asked for grape juice when cocktails were
served. She did enjoy white wine and champagne poured over ice. She was nervous
about flying and would usually drink a few glasses of champagne to calm her nerves
prior to takeoff.

Duke also enjoyed champagne, usually Dom Perignon, although any good French
or domestic label would do in a pinch. But he detested cheap vintages. One New Year's
Eve while the yacht was anchored off Mazatlán, Duke learned to his disgust that there
were only a few bottles of a mediocre, mass-market brand stored in the pantry. Billy had
forgotten to stock up on Dom Perignon before leaving Newport. This being a question
of to drink or not to drink, however, Duke gave the go-ahead to serve the inferior wine.
But he wasn't happy about it.

"Goddamn crap," he grumbled after tasting it in the galley.

•

LIKE OTHER MEN WITH A ROBUST APPETITE FOR LIFE, DUKE HAD DONE HIS SHARE OF
philandering. By his own admission he'd once been a ladies' man of epic energy.

In the days before I realized we were being seriously male chauvinistic, the crew
would hold bull sessions in the galley that sometimes took on an X-rated slant.
Although possibly more fiction than fact, the sexual bragging one day got to Floyd
Slate, our cook (Billy had not yet joined the yacht). Floyd, in his early forties, a beefy
man who wore his blond hair in a severe crewcut, sat listening to the younger men
recount their amorous adventures, a wistful look on his face. He shook his head as a
deckhand finished a tale that would have made the Marquis de Sade blush.

"I just don't seem to have the energy for the ladies like I used to," he moaned, taking the floor. "When I was younger I used to go out with a different gal every night. I used to screw all night and work all day. It never bothered me." Floyd sat at the galley table a long moment, remembering past triumphs, before continuing. "I can't do it anymore," he sighed. "I must be slowing down with age."

The rest of us—all in our early thirties or younger—commiserated on the sadness of Floyd's crumbling sexual stamina. We all agreed by age forty it was pretty much over for a man's libido. It was a moment before we noticed Duke leaning against the gunwale outside the galley's open door, watching us with an amused grin.

"Aw hell, Floyd," he said, addressing the cook but speaking to all of us. "When I was your age I was screwin' everything I could get ahold of."

I believe Duke meant this more as encouragement than boast, but the cook was unreceptive. He turned a plaintive eye toward the actor.

"Yeah, but *you're* John Wayne!"

When it came to the bedroom arts, Duke knew the *Wild Goose*'s crew was more wolf pack than band of angels. He didn't mind the lads bringing dates aboard ship while he wasn't using her, but he made it clear he didn't want the yacht turned into a floating bawdyhouse.

"I know how it is with these young bucks," he told Pete, "but I don't want things to get out of hand."

What Duke wanted and what actually happened were often two different things. Charters could be especially freewheeling. Singer Tom Jones and some musicians from

CHRIS SAUNDERS, DAUGHTER OF A FRIEND OF THE WAYNES', BALANCES ON BERT'S SHOULDERS AS TWO CREWMEN COMPLETE THE PLAYFUL TABLEAU. SUCH INNOCENT FUN WAS THE COUNTERPART TO MORE WANTON ENTERTAINMENTS THAT SOMETIMES TOOK PLACE ABOARD THE 136-FOOT YACHT. *BERT MINSHALL PHOTO*

his band once chartered the *Goose* for a trip to Ensenada, Mexico. During the voyage they did not lack for female companionship. Bikinis were busting out all over—so to speak. When the Welsh entertainer found out that most of the envious crew were single—including the Minshall brothers—he was apologetic.

"Hell," he told us, "if I'd known you guys were swingers, I'd have had the lads bring some more girls."

In the early seventies, one memorable charter turned into a floating orgy when a group of businessmen hired the yacht for a trip to San Francisco. They told the charter broker they wanted to hold a week-long "business conference" during the 450-mile voyage north. But they never said what sort of business they had in mind. The business supplies they brought aboard included several cases of booze, a batch of brownies laced with the hallucinogenic drug LSD and a half-dozen seagoing soiled doves.

By the time the *Goose* reached San Francisco, those businessmen had exhausted not only the booze but the hookers as well, while the brownies were just a mind-bending memory.

At dockside, though, awaiting our wiped-out executives, was an unpleasant surprise—their wives had learned of the yacht's carnal cargo and dispatched a delegation to greet the *Goose*. I stayed safely in the wheelhouse as the spouses conducted a spirited reunion on the dock below. As far as I know, no one was killed.

The lure of Mexico's sporting houses snared more than one of the *Goose*'s overheated crewmen. The encounters were not always without a price.

One young deckhand picked up a viral souvenir of a night spent with a local tart during liberty in Acapulco. He discovered his condition as the ship was en route to Cabo San Lucas. We kept penicillin pills in the ship's first-aid locker—but only Pete Stein had a key. The deckhand needed the pills, but he didn't want to tell the skipper why. Concocting a cover story that he had a bad "sore throat," he asked Pete for some of the antibiotics. Pete stared at him and, with the boredom of utter certainty, asked, "What's the matter? Pick up a dose of clap from one of your girlfriends?"

Duke was equally wary of his crew of budding Don Juans. One afternoon while cruising along the dry, cliff-fronted Catalina coast in the Dory, we passed a small cove a few miles northwest of Avalon. Duke, standing beside me, one hand gripping the center console for balance, inspected the cove's deserted beach and a narrow, tree-studded gorge snaking back into the hills. Suddenly, he turned to me and said, "I'd like to set up a camp for boys there and have you run it."

I was surprised and mildly terrified. I couldn't picture myself being responsible for a couple hundred high-spirited boys. I had enough trouble riding herd on the young Wayne children. But it gave me an idea.

"How about a camp for girls?" I asked.

Duke viewed me suspiciously, then shook his head.

"Hell, no," he said, dismissing the matter. "You'd get into too much trouble."

Trouble is what I nearly landed in—up to my neck—one night in 1965 while the *Goose* was anchored off Lido Isle in Newport Harbor. Duke and Pilar had returned to the ship quite late from a party ashore (remodeling work on the Bayshore estate was not yet finished, and they were spending a few days aboard ship), when they asked Ken and me to join them in the main salon for a nightcap. Soon we were sharing glasses of Dom Perignon. Duke was in rare form, very funny, telling stories that had us convulsed with laughter.

Ken eventually drifted off to bed, leaving the three of us in the salon. Not long after, Pilar excused herself, saying she wanted to get some fresh air on the afterdeck. Duke said he wanted another drink. Feeling gallant, I offered to escort Pilar aft.

Neither of us was too steady as we walked down the sidedeck. As we entered the big fantail area Pilar hesitated and I bumped into her, knocking us both off balance. We fell back onto one of the gunwale couches. Pilar landed on my lap as I instinctively put my arms around her waist to catch her.

So there I was . . . a lap full of gorgeous woman, more than a little drunk and suddenly hearing the call of the wild. Pilar giggled as we sprawled backward, unable to get up. Then I heard it for sure—not the call of the wild but the sound of footsteps coming along the sidedeck. I knew it was Duke. It was too late to untangle myself from my boss's wife. In a moment, he was standing over us, calmly taking in the scene. It couldn't have looked too good.

"C'mon, time to go to bed," he finally muttered as he reached for Pilar's arm and pulled her to her feet. Then he nudged her in the direction of the main salon. Pilar took a step forward—and fell face first onto the deck.

This was not exactly what Duke had intended. He stood there a moment, looking very surprised, then rushed to help his wife to her feet. Fortunately, Pilar escaped unhurt. To her credit she took the whole thing good-naturedly. Duke was clearly alarmed, though. He put his arm around her and together they disappeared up the sidedeck.

I was left sitting on the couch, my head swirling as it dawned on me that the cavalry had arrived in the nick of time.

Pictures and Potshots

Duke was constantly taking snapshots of his travels aboard the *Wild Goose*. He enjoyed photography and owned a variety of cameras. But there were two things about cameras that caused him considerable trouble—keeping track of them while aboard ship and trying to load them with film.

Duke could misplace a camera as easily as some people do their car keys, prompting many stem-to-stern searches of the *Goose*. And when it came to threading the film onto its winding sprocket, Duke, with his big fingers, might as well have been attempting brain surgery while wearing a baseball mitt. It wasn't until the new cartridge-loading cameras were introduced in the sixties that Duke could easily handle film-changing chores. He bought every new model that came out.

I shared Duke's enthusiasm for photography. He was always a good sport about the candid photos and home movies I took aboard ship, even when I caught him sans toupee, unshaved, with stomach protruding through his open shirt. He never seemed to mind. "I've grown too damn ugly to worry about having my picture taken," he'd joke.

Nonetheless, he knew when a camera was around. After forty years in films, he had a sixth sense about when his picture was being taken. In 1974 I visited the set of *McQ*, which was filming in Seattle. I had my Leica 35-mm with me. While waiting between camera setups, Duke spotted me and grabbed one of the film crew by the elbow. He jerked a thumb in my direction and said in a loud stage whisper, "Look out for that guy. He's a sneaky bastard with a camera!"

Duke's sense of fun usually prevailed over my sometimes intrusive lens. Once, when he spotted me filming with my 8-mm movie camera on the foredeck, he pointed at the whirring camera and began to imitate the speeded up movements of an actor in an old silent movie. (Actually, Duke got his start in films at the tail end of the silent era, appearing as an unbilled extra in three productions.) It was hilarious,

although as he shuffled back and forth across the deck he looked less like a silent film star than a mechanical bear caught in the crossfire of a shooting gallery.

I filmed him another time boarding the yacht from the Dory. When he reached the sidedeck he saw my camera. Grinning, he pushed the straw Panama-style hat he was wearing down onto his forehead and did a stylish glide along the deck. It was all surprisingly jaunty—even debonair. Duke once told friend and reporter Wayne Warga of the *Los Angeles Times*, "I always wanted to be Fred Astaire. Jeez, that guy can dance." Perhaps that's who he was pretending to be that day before my camera.

On warm nights I sometimes showed my home movies on the afterdeck for the children and guests. On occasion Duke joined us. A guest once asked how he liked "Bert's film festival."

"I haven't seen a bad scene yet," he replied. I noted the compliment—as well as the exaggeration.

Sometimes one of the children or a guest would grab my camera and start shooting. On a sunny day in Acapulco, while I was guiding Duke through one of our highly unstructured weight-lifting sessions on the boatdeck, his good friend and Newport Beach Porsche dealer Chick Iverson spotted my 8-mm on the *hickea* and decided to document the *Goose*'s first mate in action. Barbell in hand, I grinned sheepishly as the film rolled. Duke was delighted that I was getting a taste of my own medicine.

"C'mon, Bert!" he laughed. "You're a movie star, now!"

•

ANOTHER KIND OF SHOOTING THAT TOOK PLACE ABOARD SHIP HAD NOTHING TO DO WITH cameras. Duke made no secret of his enthusiasm for firearms. He kept a small shipboard arsenal locked in a closet in the captain's cabin that included shotguns and an array of small caliber rifles. He also kept a loaded .45-caliber revolver in his stateroom. Just in case. Other weapons would appear aboard ship from time to time. Duke once showed up at the Lido slip carrying a fully automatic M-16 rifle, the same kind used by U.S. troops in Vietnam. Where he got it, he never said.

On the afterdeck was a gray-painted steel box where we stored ammunition. This box doubled as a couch, complete with cushion and backrest. Guests sitting here were actually perched over hundreds of rifle and pistol rounds and shotgun shells.

With all this shipboard firepower, Duke liked to joke during our trips to Mexico that we could start a small revolution. He used the shotguns for hunting trips at various places along the Mexican coast such as Turtle Bay, about halfway down the Baja peninsula, where he once shot ducks with the town's mayor (although they turned out too salty to eat). The yacht was also set up for trap-shooting, with a spring-loaded thrower used to catapult clay targets from the stern, although Duke seldom used it.

Sharks brought out the blood lust in Duke. He believed they were a menace and did his best to dispatch as many as possible using a .22 rifle. (Today, that "see a shark, kill a shark" attitude is changing as people learn how important the predators are to the ocean's ecosystem. In fact, there's evidence that indiscriminate shooting and fishing of sharks may pose a real threat to the survival of the species around the world—information that was unknown to Duke in the sixties and seventies.)

Sometimes at night we'd shine a drop light over the side to attract small sharks. One evening off Catalina we were astonished to see the water around the yacht alive with squid. There were millions of them clogging the sea. I quickly attached a bucket to a line and dropped it overboard. When I hauled it back up it was loaded with squid, the water black as they squirted their protective ink. Although they make excellent eating when prepared correctly, Duke didn't like the looks of the tentacled, jello-like creatures and told me to dump them out.

A number of sharks also circled the yacht, feasting on the squid. Aiming the .22 at the weaving fins, Duke potted several of the predators. We watched as other sharks— attracted by the blood—began attacking their dead brothers. Within moments a full-scale feeding frenzy was under way, shark eating shark, until the water was red around the *Goose*. It was a gruesome, incredible scene.

Duke taught Ethan at an early age how to handle guns. The boy was ten when Duke bought him his own .22 rifle, complete with telescopic sight.

"Never point a weapon at anyone at any time," Duke sternly warned, then added, in a lighter tone, "Unless, of course, you mean to shoot 'em."

Although Duke stressed gun safety to Ethan, an incident occurred in 1974 that could have had tragic results.

After Pilar's separation from Duke in 1973, she moved into a home in the exclusive Big Canyon area of Newport Beach. I was talking with Marisa in the kitchen one afternoon when a large glass door opening onto the patio suddenly shattered, sending shards of glass smashing onto the tile floor. Although several small pieces hit Marisa in the legs, she was not cut. (Pilar was not home at the time, having run to the store on an errand, or I'm sure I would have had a hysterical mother on my hands.) After making sure Marisa was okay, I raced outside and saw Ethan standing on the patio holding his .22 rifle. The boy looked stunned. Apparently, ignoring his father's warnings, he'd been playing with the weapon when it accidentally discharged, sending a bullet ricocheting off the cement patio into the glass door.

Ethan was extremely upset, near tears that he might have inadvertently shot someone, and very worried about what his mother would say when she returned home. I felt sorry for the boy and told him if he promised never again to handle a gun except under the direct supervision of an adult, I'd help him out of this mess. He quickly agreed.

We concocted a story that Ethan had slipped on the patio and struck his head against the door, breaking it. It was a bit of a stretch, but Pilar on her return home was only concerned that no one had been hurt. An innately honest lad, Ethan felt bad about misleading his mother. But I told him what was done was done, and as long as he kept his promise to me, he could forget the incident and go ahead from there. Anyway, the cover-up was my responsibility—not his. The true story is out now. Perhaps I did the wrong thing. But I felt Ethan had learned his lesson. I couldn't at the time see putting him through any more agony.

Duke displayed his guns in a showcase in the den of the Bayshore house. Quite a few of the firearms were gifts from friends and various organizations. Some of the pieces were highly ornate. Lethal works of art, I suppose you could have called them.

As might be expected, Duke was a vehement foe of gun control. He vowed more than once that they'd "take my guns away over my dead body!" I'm sure his pro-gun stance helped to distance him from many of his more liberal peers in the motion-picture industry. "I'm sorry they feel that way," he'd say of those who were against private ownership of firearms. "But ya know, the first time they came across some bastard breakin' into their home or tryin' to take one of their kids, they'd be damn glad to have a gun around."

The danger of intruders was violently underscored one night when a maid at the house surprised an armed man hiding in a closet. He struck her across the side of the head with his revolver, knocking her to the floor, and then fled. Duke, in another part of the house, was alerted when the maid came to and cried for help. He grabbed the .45-caliber revolver he kept loaded on the headboard above his bed and searched the house and grounds, but found no one.

Duke was very worried about the maid, who insisted she was fine. But when she complained the next day about dizziness, Duke rushed her to a doctor. She was diagnosed as having suffered a slight concussion. Duke was much relieved when the doctor told him she'd be all right after a few days' rest.

Even now, a cold chill grips me whenever I think about what might have happened if that armed intruder had not been surprised by Duke's maid. Was he a burglar . . . or was he up to some even more sinister purpose?

Duke had always resisted turning his home into a fortress. He wasn't paranoid about some crazy walking up to his front door and pumping him full of lead. In fact, the whole family was careless about leaving the house unlocked. After the attack on his maid, though, he took steps to install an alarm system.

I sometimes worried about the threat of kidnapping when I picked the children up after school. I often played chauffeur to Ethan and Marisa, driving them between their home and the private Newport campus they attended (although, like Aissa, they later attended public high school). I even considered carrying a weapon in my car as a precaution, but decided against it as being too risky due to my inexperience with firearms.

To my knowledge, Duke suffered physical harm only once as a direct result of his ownership of guns. One morning he showed up at the yacht's slip sporting a shiner below one eye. It was a beauty. I asked him what had happened.

"Well, ya know the .45 I keep on the headboard above the bed?" he began somewhat reluctantly. "Last night while I was asleep the damn thing fell off and hit me on the cheek!"

DUKE HOLDS ONE OF THE FAMED COLT .45 REVOLVERS FROM HIS GUN COLLECTION. *BERNIE ABRAMSON PHOTO*

Sound and Fury

Pilar has written that her husband was much more prone to angry fits after his lung cancer operation in 1964. She claimed that the operation "changed him forever." That may be so. I understand that major surgeries such as the one Duke underwent can work personality changes in people. Nonetheless, on a day-to-day basis—at least while aboard the *Wild Goose*—he was most often good-natured and full of fun.

Duke had what he liked to describe as an Irish temper. Quick to erupt, then just as quick to cool off. He wasn't one to hold grudges. Once he got it out of his system, that was generally the end of it. Yet he could and did blow up with a fury that was sometimes surprising.

During one trip to Acapulco, Duke arranged for a local tailor to make him a half-dozen pairs of pants. The tailor arrived at dockside at the Club de Yates, where the *Goose* was moored, speaking little English and wearing a black beret. He measured Duke on the afterdeck using a tattered cloth tape.

Several days later the tailor returned with a stack of pants on his shoulder. Duke tried on a pair. When he reappeared in the main salon minutes later, he was furious.

"Goddamn it!" he roared. "They're too tight!" The tailor stared as Duke picked up the pile of pants from off the poker table and flung them across a couch. "Take these back and fix 'em!"

The tailor, not quite comprehending what this big angry gringo was ranting about, made no move toward the pants. Duke looked like he was about to detonate.

"Well, what the hell's the matter with you? Didn't you hear me? The fucking pants are too tight!"

I think it was the last adjective that confused the tailor. Luckily, we had an Argentine lad working aboard as steward, and Pete Stein quickly pressed him into service as translator. By the time the linguistics about the pants were cleared up, Duke had cooled down. In fact, before the tailor left, Duke had him measure the entire crew for custom swimsuits. In his own way, he was making amends for blowing his top.

"We all make mistakes," he said later, dismissing the incident.

(The altered pants were returned the next day, and this time they fit perfectly. But the crew never did get their swimsuits—we left Acapulco before they were finished. Regardless, Duke made sure that the tailor received payment for them in full.)

Another eruption of Mt. Duke took place while the *Goose* was anchored several hundred yards off actress Merle Oberon's home on Acapulco Bay. Miss Oberon, a good friend of the Waynes', had invited Duke and Pilar to a party at her spectacular, cliff-hugging mansion.

A deckhand dropped the Waynes off at a concrete landing that led up to the house. Normally he would have tied up and waited for their return, but a heavy swell kept banging the Dory into the concrete. Afraid the small boat would be damaged, he decided to return to the ship. Unfortunately, he didn't realize that Duke and Pilar now had no way back to the *Goose* except to swim. And for some reason, no arrangements were made with either Pete or me to have a boat standing by ready to pick them up. It was a complete breakdown in communications. Wars have been lost in this way.

It was a little after midnight while on anchor watch that I first heard the sound of voices drifting over the dark water. At first they were too faint to make out. Then, on a gust of wind, one broke out above the others.

"Ahoooyyyyyy on the *Wiiiiild Goooooooose* . . . ."

I ran to the gunwale. Once again, a distinct holler came out of the blackness.

"Goddamnitttttt . . . . Ahoyyyyy on the *Wiiiiiild Goooooooose* . . . ."

It was Duke. What was this all about? I wondered, racing aft. When I saw both the Whaler and the Dory tied

DUKE THROWS A CLASSIC JOHN WAYNE HAYMAKER FOR THE STOP-ACTION CAMERA. HIS REAL-LIFE FITS OF ANGER WERE SELDOM VIOLENT BUT WERE NO LESS IMPRESSIVE. *PHIL STERN PHOTO*

to the stern, I knew. He'd been left stranded ashore. I jumped into the Dory and shoved off.

As I pulled up to the landing I saw Duke waiting with several guests from the party. The thin glare from an electric light shone over the group.

"Jesus Christ!" Duke exploded, gripping the side of the Dory. "Where the hell've you been? We've been yelling for ten minutes. Why didn't you come when we called?"

"I'm sorry, Mr. Wayne, but I guess we were too far out to hear you," I said, wishing I was anywhere at that moment except in that Dory.

"C'mon, folks," he muttered, ignoring me, as he helped a pretty woman dressed in a white evening gown into the boat. Apparently, he'd invited the group back to the *Goose* for a nightcap. Pilar was still at the party.

Duke was doing his best to control himself as we shoved off, but I could tell he was livid. "It damn well isn't fair! It damn well isn't fair!" he kept repeating.

Once out on the water, though, he suddenly calmed down. He turned in his seat and began joking with his guests. It was as if someone had pulled the burning fuse from a bundle of dynamite.

On our return to the ship I woke Pete Stein and told him what had happened. "We're sure as hell not going to leave Pilar high and dry, too," he grumbled, roaring off in the Whaler while I stayed in the Dory at the *Goose*. Between the two of us we made sure a ready shuttle service was available between ship and shore in either direction.

The next morning Pete made an unscheduled trip into Acapulco, returning a few hours later with two packages. He unwrapped them and took out two battery-powered walkie-talkie radios—something of a novelty in the mid-1960s.

"From now on we'll give one of these to whoever's going ashore," he explained. "When they want to return, they can let us know." Pete handed me the two radios, with the satisfied look of a man who had just pulled the fuse from the dynamite.

He didn't look so smug, however, the day at Catalina when an unauthorized booze run into Avalon nearly got him kicked off the *Wild Goose* for good.

I made the mistake of going along with him, intending to see a girlfriend in town. I left Ethan and Aissa on the beach at White's Cove in care of a deckhand as Pete and I raced off in the Whaler toward Avalon, respectively in search of J&B scotch and a pretty island youth camp counselor named Barbara.

We both found what we were looking for. An hour later, once again back in the Whaler, me with memories of Barbara dancing in my head and Pete with a case of scotch secured in the bow, we cast off for the return trip.

We should have high-tailed it back to the *Goose* because we were already technically AWOL. But at the harbor entrance Pete spotted a familiar-looking vessel—the two-masted schooner *Goodwill*. This was the same ship whose bowsprit the *Goose* had snagged two years earlier at Cabo San Lucas. When Pete spotted the *Goodwill's* skipper, an old friend named Flink, walking on deck, he decided a detour was in order.

I spent the next two hours listening to a classic exchange of nautical blarney as Pete and Flink locked in verbal *mano a mano* in the *Goodwill's* salon. Both men were in rare form, fueled by glasses of scotch. I'm certain some of their tales were even true, such as the time Flink rounded the Horn on one of the last clipper ships, or how he survived a torpedoing by a German U-boat while serving on a freighter during convoy duty in the North Atlantic. It was after five o'clock when we finally stood up to go. We shook hands with the venerable Captain Flink and started back up the coast.

(A tragic note concerning the *Goodwill*—in 1969 Pete and I learned that the big steel-hulled schooner was lost with all hands after breaking up on the Sacramento Reef off Baja California. Captain Flink was not aboard, having retired from active service by then. Call it sailor's superstition or a flair for the dramatic, but Pete claimed it was no coincidence that the schooner was carrying a crew of thirteen when she went down.)

On our arrival at the *Goose*, Pete told me to go topside and make ready to hoist the ship's tenders onto the boatdeck. (We were due to return to Newport Beach after dinner.) Duke was sitting in a chair next to the *hickea* playing cards with Pilar and several friends when I poked my head through the hatch that led from the afterdeck. Duke looked at me but said nothing as the others continued their game.

When Pete showed up to help me secure the boats in their cradles, Duke suddenly threw his cards on the *hickea* and stood up, pushing the chair back along the deck. He raised his right arm and pointed a thick index finger at Pete. No one moved. For a moment it looked like a wax tableau from Madame Tussaud's in London.

"Skipper!" he bellowed, still pointing. "You and I are *through*!"

Instantly I knew what was behind Duke's fury. I'd been thinking about it on the way back, that we'd been gone a long time, and that the deckhand I'd left at White's with the children had probably told Duke why we'd gone into town. I didn't blame him for that. We hadn't tried to make any secret of it. Now Pete had been canned for what Duke considered dereliction of duty. I felt certain my head was next on the block. But still Duke said nothing to me.

Later I found Pete sitting alone in the wheelhouse, shaking his head and staring out at the darkening water. As crusty as he seemed, Pete nonetheless loved serving aboard the *Wild Goose*. He admired Duke and was loyal to him. He was close to tears.

"I guess I loused up the best thing that ever happened to me," he said when he saw me, his voice breaking.

I sat down to dinner in the galley, but my appetite was shot. It wasn't long before one of the deckhands arrived with word that Duke wanted to see me on the boatdeck. I expected the worst. Well, I thought, getting up from the table, Liverpool here I come.

Duke was standing alone near the Whaler when I arrived.

"You wanted to see me, Mr. Wayne?" My stomach was doing acrobatics. Duke leaned against the skiboat, a relaxed figure in the gathering dusk.

"I want you to know that I heard about your goofing off today," he said quietly. "Is it true you went into town to see a girlfriend?"

My stomach suddenly did a triple somersault. "Yes, sir," I confessed. He stepped forward and put a hand on my shoulder. "Bert, you can have your fun when you're off duty. But when I'm using the yacht, I expect you to do your job."

"I'm sorry, Mr. Wayne. It won't happen again." I meant it.

"I know it won't," he said. He let loose of my shoulder. "You can go back to your dinner now."

Relief swept over me as I walked back to the galley. It was tempered, however, by the knowledge that my good luck had not helped Pete.

It was close to midnight when we pulled into the slip at Lido Anchorage. Pete had piloted the big yacht home for the last time. Because of the late hour Duke and Pilar decided to spend the night aboard ship and return home in the morning. I, for one, spent a fitful night's sleep. I felt lousy about Pete's getting the boot, and I suppose guilty that I hadn't.

Early the next morning Pete was in the galley drinking coffee. Judging by his numb stare, hemlock would have been more appropriate. I poured a cup and sat down. We didn't say much. Gloom hung heavy in the air. Pete finally roused himself to tell me he would wait to pack his sea chest until after the Waynes left the ship.

"Jesus, Bert," he said, dejected. "I can't believe this has happened."

As we sat there in silent mourning, I heard footsteps approaching along the side-deck. A moment later Duke stepped through the galley's open door. He ducked his head to avoid the overhang. "Mornin'," he said, heading for the coffee pot. "Thought I'd let you know we're about ready to go."

Pete started to rise from his seat. Duke motioned him to sit down. "Finish your coffee, Skipper." Pete was silent as the actor filled a large ceramic mug from the pot and took a quick sip.

With Duke's entrance Pete had automatically assumed his traditional shipboard poker face. A proud man, I knew he'd never let Duke see how upset he was or beg him for another chance. He managed to look detached, his eyelids drooping low. As if he was about to nod off at any moment. Duke wasn't the only good actor aboard ship.

But as Duke headed out the galley door, he paused.

"By the way, Skipper," he said, turning back. "We had a pretty good time this weekend. Have the boat ready so we can go back to the island next week."

Pete's eyelids slowly rose.

Duke gave a wave of his hand and disappeared around the bulkhead. We could hear his footsteps fading off along the deck.

Pete absently picked up his coffee cup. His hand shook visibly. He quickly set the cup back down. It rattled against the table top as he let loose. He knew I'd seen it.

"Not a word, Bert," he cautioned. Then he stood up and strode from the galley, a forgiven man.

Yardbird

Pete Stein always remained a great favorite of Duke's, no matter the mischief he stirred up for himself or the *Wild Goose*. As Duke once kiddingly told him, "Pete, when they make a movie of your life, *I* want to play the lead."

Things just seemed to happen to Pete. Like the first day the *Goose* arrived in Newport Harbor and proceeded to literally drop anchor when a connecting link in the chain parted and five hundred pounds of iron broke free. Only bare chain was left dangling out the hawsepipe in the bow. The anchor was gone, buried in the bottom muck of the bay. At the same time, the gearshifts momentarily stuck, sending the yacht nose-first into a sandbar off Lido Isle—almost directly opposite Duke's new home. None of this was Pete's fault, but it was still an embarrassing way to make a debut. (Pete later hired divers and a floating crane to retrieve the anchor.) Duke, on one of his first visits to the ship following his lung cancer operation, teased the skipper about the mishap, saying loudly that when Pete decided to drop anchor, he made "damn sure it was dropped!"

BERT AND SKIPPER PETE STEIN DRESSED AS PIRATES FOR A SEGMENT OF THE *TARZAN* TELEVISION SERIES THAT WAS FILMED ABOARD THE *GOOSE* IN THE LATE 1960S. *BERT MINSHALL PHOTO*

Pete had a streak of pirate running through him, a holdover from his days sailing a rumrunner during Prohibition. In one of the *Goose*'s more infamous episodes, Pete once "unknowingly" helped a friend smuggle thousands of dollar's worth of furniture and appliances into Mexico, a ploy to avoid paying duty on the items. The yacht was crammed with refrigerators, televisions, furniture and dozens of boxes containing everything from silverware to bedspreads. It was all destined for a hotel Pete's friend was building in Acapulco.

I was nervous as hell on the trip down, but we made the resort city without incident. Like a scene out of a spy movie, we arrived at our rendezvous point in the dead of night, the *Goose*'s running lights and portholes blacked out on Pete's orders. Waiting in the dark were three fast powerboats and their silent crews. We worked by flashlight, everyone creeping around, transporting the boxes and appliances into shore where more silent men received them. I couldn't believe it was happening. Not aboard John

Wayne's yacht, of all vessels. Thankfully, the operation went smoothly, and we were soon sailing back to our Club de Yates slip.

(I subsequently learned from Pete that the items were taken to a house belonging to a high-ranking ex-official of the Mexican government. An informant later ratted to customs officials, who fined Pete's friend forty thousand dollars. Pete's guardian angel must have been working overtime, because his role in the scheme never surfaced.)

I always got along well with Pete. I enjoyed his colorful stories and his deadpan humor. In the late sixties we even made our "screen debuts" together—playing pirate extras when a segment of the old *Tarzan* television series featuring Ron Ely was filmed aboard the *Goose*. Pete looked especially pirate-like with his swarthy skin, dark eyes and mustache. Duke later claimed that the skipper was only playing himself.

Although Duke and I agreed there was a charm to Pete's sometimes crusty personality, there were those whom the skipper could and did rub the wrong way.

In 1965 the yacht spent several days on charter off Catalina with singer Dean Martin and his family. Dean, a close pal and occasional co-star of Duke's (they made *The Sons of Katie Elder* and *Rio Bravo* together), was as friendly and relaxed as he appeared in his movies and on television. He and his son, Dino (who later died in a National Guard jet fighter crash), spent most of the time fishing and shooting trap from the yacht's stern.

When we returned to the Lido slip at the conclusion of the trip, Ken and I walked out to the parking lot with the Martins to say good-bye. But as we talked we were soon interrupted by the ship's steward racing up the dock.

"You guys better go fish the skipper outta the drink!" he shouted as he sprinted past. Dean raised an eyebrow.

"Now what the hell was that all about?" he wondered, looking after the rapidly retreating steward.

We hurried back to the yacht in time to see Pete Stein thrashing about in the bay. As a highly amused Dean Martin looked on, Ken and I helped our waterlogged skipper onto the dock.

"That wise guy," was all he could manage at first as he tried to catch his breath.

From habit Pete fumbled in his shirt pocket for a cigarette. The pack was soaked. Dean flipped him one from his own pack.

"Here, Captain," he said. "It's not your brand, but it's drier." Pete lit the cigarette off Dean's lighter and took a deep drag. It wasn't long before we got the story behind his unexpected swim.

"It's because that damn steward was goofing off during the trip," Pete explained. "I called him on it when we got back to the slip and he threw me off the boatdeck! That wise guy," mut-

tered the soggy skipper once more, much to Dean's delight.

We never saw the steward again. He disappeared, leaving his few belongings behind in the crew's quarters. He probably thought he'd drowned old Pete.

One person who took special satisfaction in the skipper's involuntary high dive was Dean Martin.

Pete's sometimes brusque manner had irritated the crooner.

"Ya know, Bert," he confided before getting into his limousine for the trip back to his home in Los Angeles, "I'd like to have done the same thing myself!"

In the spring of 1969, during an evening charter with a group of businessmen and their wives, Pete came as close to sinking the *Goose* as he ever got, when he ran her onto a submerged jetty off the entrance to San Diego Harbor.

Although the jetty was marked with navigation lights, Pete had somehow failed to see them. We were stuck tight, hung up amidships on the jetty's sharp rocks. During a quick inspection trip below, I found several holes the size of my fist punched in the *Goose*'s three-inch-thick Douglas fir hull. Seawater was gushing into the aft bilges, although for the moment the pumps seemed to be holding the flow.

Pete was understandably reluctant to call the Coast Guard for help. He instead tried to free the ship by working the gearshifts back and forth. But she wouldn't budge.

Meanwhile, on the afterdeck, our guests huddled in small groups, talking nervously and looking very worried. The deckhands were trying to keep everyone calm. One of the businessmen—who no doubt had seen too many movies about sea disasters on the late show—commandeered the bar set up near the aft bulkhead and started pouring drinks, shouting out, "C'mon, folks! Nothin' to worry about!"

It was a noble effort, but when I ordered the deckhands to break out the lifejackets, the guests suspected there was plenty to worry about.

We must have stayed on that jetty at least a half-hour before Pete gave up and radioed the Coast Guard. He had no choice. The *Goose* was rolling heavily in the swells. I could see bits of ship's timber floating along the hull in the decklights as the rocks continued to grind into the keel and bilges, widening the holes already there. The pumps were in danger of being overwhelmed. If the lower compartments flooded, we'd have to abandon ship.

I felt sorry for Pete as the Coast Guard cutter with the familiar orange stripe on its bow hove into view, ready to pass us a towline. I realized as well as he that there was now no way he could avoid an official board of inquiry into the accident.

The *Goose* was hurt, but she wasn't mangled . . . yet. As the yacht was dragged bow first across the rocks, her props and rudders were seriously damaged. Ken shut down the engines as violent shaking wracked both propeller shafts. We had lost all steering. Seawater continued to pour into the aft bilges, straining the pumps.

Early the next morning the *Goose* was put into emergency drydock at a local shipyard—the same shipyard where several days earlier her bottom had been cleaned and painted during routine maintenance. When the shipyard workers saw the yacht sitting high and dry on the ways the next morning, they were shocked. She was a sorry sight. Most of her keel was torn away. She looked like a giant fish whose backbone had been ripped out. Several jagged holes the size of grapefruit were gouged in the bilge planks. Both props were bent beyond repair, one propeller shaft was shattered, and the five-inch-thick, solid-brass rudderposts were twisted forty-five degrees out of true. All told, it would take six weeks of labor and $70,000 to repair the damage (the same repairs today would cost well over $150,000).

The shipyard workers teased Pete unmercifully about his bad luck. They rechristened the yacht the *Yardbird*, in honor of her recent penchant for roosting in drydock. Some of the charter guests, fully recovered from their close call, returned to present Pete with a special trophy to commemorate the accident—a horse's rear end mounted on a wood pedestal. The workers roared when they saw it. Pete, to his credit, accepted the trophy with a grin.

Seawater was still dripping from the hull when the local television and newspaper people learned of the mishap and descended on the shipyard. Pete offered some fairly succinct answers to the reporters' questions. The first and most obvious question: What happened? Pete stared calmly into the TV cameras.

"Guess I zigged when I should have zagged," he drawled. It was as good an explanation as any.

But when Duke arrived a couple of days later to inspect the damage, I knew Pete would have to do some fast talking to get himself out of this one.

Duke showed up about mid-morning in his Pontiac station wagon, along with his friend Ernie Saftig. (Ernie, a former San Diego cop and PT boat commander during World War II, first met Duke during the filming of *They Were Expendable*, having been hired by director John Ford as a technical expert for the film's PT boat scenes.) I was on the bow attending to touch-up painting on the anchor windlass as Duke, a yachting

THE *WILD GOOSE* UNDERGOING REPAIRS AND MAINTENANCE IN DRYDOCK. *BERT MINSHALL PHOTO*

cap pulled low over his forehead, descended the ramp to the drydock floor.

It had to have been a tough twenty minutes Pete spent as he walked with the two men in a slow tour of the *Goose*'s battered carcass. Pete did most of the talking while Duke listened. The actor occasionally stopped to peer under the hull, his hands shoved in his front pockets, not saying a word.

I stopped painting when I heard them coming up the starboard side. They rounded the bow and turned for one final look. Duke stood with his legs apart, staring at the ship.

"Skipper," I heard him say, "I do not know, and maybe I do not *want* to know, about what you have been telling me." He spoke deliberately, emphasizing each word. "But I *would* like to use that boat. Get her fixed as soon as you can."

That was it. He turned and walked back to the ramp, Ernie bringing up the rear. Pete looked more surprised than relieved.

I admit I was astonished. Pete had escaped without so much as a verbal reprimand. And then it happened.

Duke stepped on the ramp and glanced back at the yacht, then looked directly at me. I was still standing at the bowrail, a paintbrush in one hand, a bucket in the other, when he raised his arm and pointed, his voice rumbling across the shipyard.

"FILL YOUR HANDS, YOU SONOFABITCH!"

All work around the yard came to an instant halt as men turned to see who was about to be murdered. I was fighting to get my heart going again when Duke suddenly grinned, put his head back, and let out a roar of laughter. Although I didn't know it at the time, I'd just been bellowed at with a line from *True Grit*, a film Duke had recently completed. But obviously the whole thing was a joke—on me. I pointed the brush at him like a six-shooter and called out that I had him covered.

"Like hell!" he shouted back. Then, with a wave of his hand, he strode in his best movie walk up the ramp to his waiting station wagon.

When I later saw *True Grit* in the theater I nearly came out of my seat when Duke's character, Marshal Rooster Cogburn, confronts three mounted gunmen across a mountain meadow and shouts his challenge after being taunted as a "one-eyed fatman." It was the line he yelled at me that day in the shipyard. I thought it was a magnificent scene as Duke, the reins of his horse gripped between clenched teeth, a revolver in one hand and a rifle in the other, rides hell-bent-for-glory straight toward the three desperados who were foolish enough to insult a man with grit. I was thrilled that Duke had given me a tiny connection with one of his greatest screen moments.

And how typical of Duke's loyalty to Pete Stein and his sense of humor that he not only forgave Pete for running the *Wild Goose* onto that jetty, but refused to allow the incident to ruin his pleasure in a good-natured joke.

ETHAN JOINS HIS FATHER IN A MINIATURE VERSION OF MARSHAL ROOSTER T. COGBURN ON THE SET OF *TRUE GRIT*. PHIL STERN PHOTO

Sailing before the Storm

Much has been written about Duke's politics. Sometimes his critics had trouble separating the man from his political beliefs.

The Vietnam War raised Duke's political blood pressure, although it wasn't until he toured the battle area in 1966 at the request of the U.S. State Department that he formed any strong opinions concerning the Southeast Asian conflict. When he returned it was obvious he'd been profoundly affected by what he'd seen. He came to believe that the war was a desperate struggle between democracy and the archenemy of mankind—communism. It had suddenly become highly personal to him.

He brought back dozens of plaques from the combat units he'd visited. All were inscribed with appreciation to John Wayne. He had me screw them onto the bulkheads around the main salon and above the *hickea*. Others he kept in his den at home.

I once overheard him discussing the war with a group of close friends that included his co-star from *Stagecoach*, Claire Trevor, and her husband, Milton Bren. This was about the time he directed the controversial *Green Berets*. Duke told them that he was all for "going in there [Vietnam] and getting it over with." He was clearly frustrated by what he perceived to be the no-win policy adopted by Washington.

"God, how I hate all this political pussyfooting around," he lamented.

But Duke still threw his support to those politicians in whom he believed. On separate occasions he'd had Ronald Reagan and Richard Nixon as breakfast guests aboard the *Wild Goose*. Nor was he averse to turning the yacht over to various political organizations for fund-raising events—all conservative, needless to say.

Yet Duke could show a surprising disinterest in the events to which he lent his name and physical presence. During a shipboard fund-raiser in Marina Del Rey (a posh

DUKE SIGNS AUTOGRAPHS FOR THREE SOUTH VIETNAMESE GIRLS DURING A 1966 TRIP TO SAIGON. LOOKING OVER HIS SHOULDER IS HIS MILITARY ESCORT, CAPT. PETE DAWKINS. *UPI/BETTMANN*

harbor community fifty miles up the coast from Newport), Duke attended the function
in a dutiful attempt to help the organizers, but he spent most of the evening glued to
the television set in the master stateroom—watching a USC football game.

Actually, Duke liked to think of himself as a true independent in his politics. He
claimed his approach to issues was to study all sides, then make up his mind whether to
lend his support or not. It's just that his approach usually took a turn to the right somewhere along the way. One notable exception was when he backed Democratic President Jimmy Carter on the treaty to turn the Panama Canal over to Panama. As he said
later, "Man, I sure caught hell [from the conservatives] on that one." But he never
backed down from his belief that the treaty was fair and honorable.

In 1967 Duke made *The War Wagon* with Kirk Douglas. The two actors were at
opposite ends of the political spectrum. At the time, Ronald Reagan was running for
governor of California. Douglas opposed Reagan, while Duke thought the future president was the greatest. There were spirited exchanges between the two actors, both on
and off the set, although Duke, who always professed a liking and respect for Douglas,
later insisted they were "friendly disagreements."

When I saw *The War Wagon* shortly after its release, I thought the two men made a
good team. I later asked Duke what he thought of his co-star and sometime political
adversary. He thought a moment before replying.

"Aw," drawled Duke, "he tries too hard."

I never asked him if he was referring to Douglas's politics or his acting.

•

IN THE SUMMER OF 1969, KEN AND I WERE VISITED BY OUR PARENTS. I WAS ANXIOUS TO
show them the *Wild Goose*. I thought our father, who had served forty years as chief
steward on Manx ferryboats running between Liverpool and the Isle of Man, would be
especially interested in the ship.

Dad was a small man, a dapper dresser who always wore a Homburg on his daily
walks about Wallasey, no-nonsense but never harsh with any of his five sons. When
Ken had first asked me to join the *Goose*'s crew, our father doubted that I'd stick with
it. "You'll be back," he said at the time.

But now he knew that I'd found a new home here in America. A couple of months earlier Ken and I had moved off the ship and bought a mobile home in a Costa Mesa trailer park. As far as I was concerned, my English roots had taken firm hold in the California soil.

Although Duke was flying out of town that day on business, he graciously told Ken and me to bring our folks over to the Bayshore house for a visit. He gave them a grand welcome and then a guided tour of the house. He was already behind schedule, but he never hurried us or gave our parents the impression that their visit was anything but the most important event of his day.

Out on the patio Duke posed for snapshots, as well as 8-mm movies, with Mom and Dad. Our parents were thrilled, even Dad, who was generally reserved and very English proper. By now Duke was running quite late. However, he took a few more minutes to chat with our folks in the hot sunshine on the patio. As he excused himself he told them, "Mr. and Mrs. Minshall, you have two fine boys there."

Mom and Dad beamed as Duke shook hands and then hurried off to make his flight. Privately, Ken and I appreciated Duke's thoughtfulness in making our parents' visit memorable.

After dinner that night our father made, for him, a strong endorsement of our boss. "Nice fellow," he said, nodding his head.

·

DUKE WAS A POWERFUL, RESPONSIBLE MAN, BUT NOT TOO FAR BELOW THE SURFACE WAS the little boy waiting to leap out and stick a lighted match in the sole of your shoe. His enthusiasms were big and his pleasures many. Sometimes the simplest things gave him the greatest amusement.

Duke liked to fish from the *Goose*'s stern, dropping a line over the side, content to pass an entire afternoon this way. Bait was kept in a freezer along the gunwale, although sometimes we kept live anchovies in the saltwater tank bolted to the center of the afterdeck. The children thought this red-painted tank with round windows was an aquarium.

One afternoon while the *Goose* was anchored in a cove near Acapulco, I came across Duke bending over this tank. At first I thought he was only trying to corral another anchovy for his hook, but through one of the tank's windows I saw gripped in his submerged hand a small rubber shark that he had bought for his children in Acapulco. I watched as he maneuvered the shark in a mock attack on the anchovies. Whether the fish were panicked by the little rubber predator or by the big arm holding it, there was an underwater stampede as Duke chased them with his Jaws, Jr.

Duke was laughing the whole time, his short-sleeved shirt soaked to the shoulder as water splashed over the tank's rim onto the deck. I retreated to the sidedeck before he spotted me. I didn't want to spoil his fun.

Gadgets fascinated Duke. I once helped him rig a small electric hoist with a fishing

BERT'S FATHER, ALBERT MIN-SHALL, WHO SERVED FORTY YEARS WITH THE WORLD'S OLDEST FERRY-BOAT LINE, THE ISLE OF MAN STEAM PACKET COMPANY, DRESSED IN HIS CHIEF STEWARD'S UNIFORM.

line, to which we attached a weighted leader with a half-dozen hooks. All Duke had to do to raise or lower the line was to hit the power switch. He planned to use the device to catch small sand dabs off Catalina. Duke loved the tiny fish fried in batter for breakfast. He could eat a dozen or more at a sitting.

"This thing is gonna wipe out every sand dab within ten miles," he laughed the first time he used it, watching from the boarding ladder as the line traveled over a pulley and down into the water.

The contraption worked magnificently, pulling up sometimes as many as four or five wriggling fish at a time. Duke tried to increase the catch by adding even more hooks. He attached so many that he had trouble baiting them all—he kept sticking his big fingers with the tiny barbs.

For more than a decade that hoist performed its fish-catching duties in the waters off Catalina. Sometimes there'd be so many fat dabs hanging from the line that it would snap under the strain, plunging leader and fish back into the sea.

The first time this happened Duke glared at me and pointed an accusing finger.

"That was *your* breakfast!" he growled—then happily set about attaching another leader and hooks to the broken line.

•

FOR YEARS DUKE WAS INFATUATED WITH MAIL-ORDER CATALOGS. AS A KID HIS FOLKS had been too poor to order anything from the catalogs that sometimes passed through his home. Duke vowed that if someday he made a lot of money, he'd order any and everything that caught his eye. And that's just what he did.

Duke would browse through catalogs by the hour, marking all the merchandise he wanted. Then he'd ask his secretary, Mary St. John, to write the appropriate checks and send away for the items.

Quite often when I visited the house, Duke would have accumulated boxes of mail-order goods for me to haul back to the *Wild Goose* for storage. The gadgets and novelties passing through the Wayne household seemed endless. Brass paperweights, nautical seat cushions, kitchen slicers-and-dicers, racks to hold everything from shoes to kitchen spices (many of which I assembled), tiny hand-held cooling fans powered by batteries—you name it, and Duke had ordered it. Sometimes two and three at a time.

Duke was especially fond of flashlights. He couldn't get enough of them. I often thought that at any time I could rummage through one of those boxes and find enough flashlights to equip an entire Boy Scout troop for a night hike.

We'd keep the items at the yacht for awhile but would eventually end up giving most of them to friends or local charities. What we didn't give away more often than not ended up in "Billy's closet." (This phantom closet was the repository over the years of numerous items not wanted around ship. Whenever Billy Sweatt

DUKE POINTS THE WAY AS BERT AND PATRICK WAYNE (SECOND FROM RIGHT) MAN THE PADDLES. IN THE STERN IS DUKE'S FRIEND, FORMER PT BOAT SKIPPER ERNIE SAFTIG. *BERT MINSHALL PHOTO*

would come across something that was about to be discarded, he'd invariably grab it and say, "This is going in Billy's closet." He must have put together quite a collection of *Wild Goose* memorabilia over the years.)

Duke never asked what became of all those mail-order treasures. Mary told me he didn't seem to care. To him the fun came in searching through the catalogs. Once the check was mailed, she explained, he tended to lose interest.

Duke's children often provided a handy excuse for fun. He'd join them in the galley or on the afterdeck for a game of Monopoly, or spend hours swimming and playing water games with them off the yacht's stern.

Duke early on urged me to teach the children respect for the sea. He wanted them to approach the water with a sense of caution. I may have taught them too well. For years they absolutely refused to enter the water until I dove in first, on the theory that if any sharks were lurking about, I would attract them. If I survived uneaten, they'd happily dive in after me.

Often, when Duke first entered the water, he would glide submerged for a way, then break the surface and loudly exclaim, "Jeezus Christ, it's cold!" The children would always laugh and giggle, diving in to show their thin-skinned father just how warm it was.

"You kids are too tough for me," Duke would say, treading water as his youngsters splashed about.

One of the children's favorite games was "Let's Dunk Daddy!" They'd clamber onto Duke's shoulders, grabbing onto his bald head, sometimes inadvertently sticking a small finger in his ear or eye, each trying to be king of the floating mountain. The whole time Duke would be laughing so hard he'd usually end up choking on a mouthful of seawater.

I was swimming with him and the kids one afternoon while the yacht was anchored off Catalina, when he spotted Billy Sweatt on the fantail getting in an hour's fishing. He grabbed hold of the swimstep and motioned me to join him.

"Listen, Bert," he said in a conspiratorial tone. "Can you hold your breath long enough to dive under the keel of the boat?" I told him I thought I could.

"Good," he said, sliding a swim mask over to me. "Put this on and go down and give Billy's line a good yank. He'll think he's hooked Moby Dick."

As Duke treaded water in order to catch the look on Billy's face, I swallowed as much air as my lungs could hold and dove beneath the ship. It took me a moment to spot Billy's thin fishing line. I swam forward, gripped it with both hands, and yanked hard. I may have yanked a little too hard. Suddenly, slicing through the water in front of me like a spear, shot Billy's fishing pole. I was so surprised that I let go of the line. The pole sank quickly out of reach into the depths below. I'd pulled it right out of Billy's hands.

When I broke the surface I looked up and saw Billy peering over the side, dumbfounded. Duke was beside himself with hilarity.

"Bert, you just cost me a hundred dollars," he roared, referring to the cost of the pole and reel, "but it was worth it!"

Another time *I* was the object of Duke's unrestrained enjoyment. The *Goose* was anchored off Coyote Bay one afternoon as I was engaged in an impromptu diving exhibition for the children. Duke was up the coast in the Boston Whaler getting in a few hours' fishing. Pilar had gone along to keep him company. It was a blistering hot day. Aissa and Ethan watched from the boatdeck railing as several of us in the crew took turns plunging into the sea. Time and again we dove into the cool, incredibly clear water. It was marvelous.

I had rigged up a makeshift diving board on the bow by jamming a ten-foot piece of wood planking under the drum of the anchor windlass. It made a fair springboard. I was

MARISA, READY FOR AN AFTER-
NOON'S WATERSKIING, SITS ON THE
PLYWOOD SLED BERT BUILT FOR
THE WAYNE CHILDREN. *BERT MIN-
SHALL PHOTO*

having a good day and felt cocky. I was prime for some showing off when I spotted Duke and Pilar returning in the Whaler. As they drew close I started my hop step onto the plank. I never made it to the end of the board. There was the sharp crack of break-ing wood as the plank gave way. I dropped like a man stepping on a trapdoor, hitting the water in a spectacular bellyflop.

I was stunned for a moment but struggled back to the surface, my face, chest and stomach stinging from the impact. I felt as if I'd been belted with a dozen wet towels. When I cleared the water from my eyes I could see the Whaler drifting a few feet away. Duke was standing at the controls, convulsed with laughter.

"Gee, Bert!" he shouted gleefully. "I wish *I* could do that!"

•

IN 1970 DUKE WON THE BEST ACTOR OSCAR FOR HIS SWAGGERING PORTRAYAL OF THE boozing, one-eyed Marshal Rooster Cogburn in *True Grit*. It was bloody well about time, I thought, as I watched the Academy Awards show on television. I was proud and happy for him. I was no longer a lukewarm John Wayne fan. I'd wanted him to win. I watched as he made his acceptance speech. He was overcome with emotion. (I later read that this Oscar telecast was the highest rated in the show's history.)

It was several weeks before I saw Duke's Oscar in person. Duke had been away on location filming *Rio Lobo*. He wanted to display the award on the trophy shelf in his den. But when he set it down among the dozens of other awards and plaques, it was overwhelmed by the clutter.

"Lookit that," he said, standing back. "There's too much other stuff around it. Do you think you could put a higher base on it so it'll stick up above the rest?"

I picked up the statuette. It had the heft of a dumbbell. I told him I thought I could fix up something that would work.

The next morning I drove to a local trophy shop where I purchased a black plastic pedestal I thought would do the job. I had Duke's Oscar out in my car. It seemed odd driving around town with John Wayne's Academy Award covered by a blanket in the back seat. Back at the Lido slip I fastened the pedestal to the statuette in my woodworking shop. It added about three inches to its height. I could have used an even taller base, but I didn't want Duke's golden friend to look as if he were astride Mt. Olympus.

"Hey, that's pretty good," said Duke when I showed it to him. He cleared a spot for the award on the shelf. He was quite pleased with the effect of the higher base.

Not long after I modified the actor's Academy Award, he showed up at the Lido berth carrying a large manila folder. He opened it and slid the contents out onto the galley table.

"Here, I want you to put this on the side somewhere."

Lying on the table was a sheet of gold foil cut in the shape of an Oscar. It was pre-glued on the back.

That gold decal reminded me of how warships marked themselves during World War II whenever their guns shot down an enemy plane or sank a hostile ship. Only in

DUKE, HOLDING HIS BEST ACTOR OSCAR FOR *TRUE GRIT*, GETS A CONGRATULATORY KISS FROM PRE-SENTER BARBRA STREISAND. *UPI/BETTMANN* this case, Duke's "kill" was being named Best Actor. I applied the full-sized foil Oscar to the yacht's side just forward of the boarding ladder. Those embarking couldn't miss it.

But there was something different about this Oscar. Across its gold face was painted a black eye-patch—Duke's amusing tribute to the fellow who'd made it all possible.

•

IT WAS A WINTER AFTERNOON IN EARLY 1970, several months before Duke won his Oscar for portraying the "one-eyed fatman." I was standing beside my boss on a Catalina hillside overlooking Avalon. In the distance, down in the harbor, we could see one of the famous glassbottom boats that explore the island's beautiful underwater reefs. Duke was telling me about the fishing off Catalina in the old days.

"Zane Grey used to catch some really huge marlin off here back in the twenties," he was saying. "The seas around here were loaded with 'em. Not any more. All fished out. It's a damned shame."

He shook his head as he recalled the glory days of Catalina marlin fishing.

"Say, you know who Zane Grey was, don't ya?" He didn't wait for a reply. "Hell of a good Western writer."

Duke was in high spirits. We'd rented a tiny jeep-like vehicle in Avalon and were using it to explore the roads that wound through the hills above the small resort town. Ethan and Marisa were with us. It had been a wonderful weekend at the island, and we'd be heading back to Newport Beach later that night. It must have been the unusually warm winter sunshine, but I found myself blurting out, "This is the kind of day that makes you glad to be alive!"

I was instantly embarrassed, but Duke, peering into the distance as a wind rose up fresh and cool from the sea, agreed.

"It sure is," he said simply.

It was getting late when we finally shoved off in the British Dory for the trip back to the *Goose*, which was anchored up the coast at White's Cove. Duke was ready for dinner. Steak and potatoes. His usual. Fifteen minutes later, as we rounded a point of jagged rock, the big yacht came into view.

"Okay, Bert, let's take her on home," said Duke, spotting the ship. I revved the motor, and the Dory raced toward the aging minesweeper gently rolling at anchor in the deepening twilight.

Neither Duke nor I realized that a particularly carefree period in both our lives was drawing to a close on that lovely winter day off Catalina. More than six years had passed since I'd joined the *Wild Goose* on a hot afternoon in Barcelona. They'd been years of unsurpassed enjoyment.

We would never see quite their like again.

Sea Change

In the spring of 1970 Captain Pete Stein died of a massive heart attack. Although only in his early sixties, Pete had had a history of heart trouble since suffering a mild coronary in 1964. After that first attack his doctors tried to persuade him to quit cigarettes. But he remained a heavy smoker until the day he died.

The *Wild Goose* was in Mazatlán when Pete collapsed at his home in the Corona Del Mar area of Newport Beach. He'd flown back to California several days earlier to testify at the U.S. Coast Guard board of inquiry called to investigate the yacht's grounding off San Diego the previous year. After spending a nervous day answering the board's questions, the skipper went home, lit a cigarette, and died. He was buried at Pacific View Memorial Park overlooking Newport Beach.

Before Pete left the yacht for California he had a long talk with Duke about the upcoming hearing. He was understandably distraught about facing the inquiry board. He was certain that he'd lose his captain's license. Duke assured him that he would back him on this.

"No matter what happens," he told the worried skipper, "the *Goose* will always be your ship, Pete."

Still, the skipper was in a somber mood when he left for Newport. Duke later speculated that the stress of the hearing simply proved too much for him. "Wouldn't ya know it that ol' Pete would beat the rap by dying," he said with sad irony.

The mood aboard ship reminded me of the time we lost the three boys that awful

CAPTAIN PETE STEIN AND HIS CLASSIC THUNDERBIRD SPORTS CAR SHORTLY BEFORE HIS DEATH. *BERT MINSHALL PHOTO*

night off Baja. Duke was very down. He had great affection for the crusty skipper. He had always turned a kind eye on Pete's shenanigans. Now the long career of one of Newport Beach's most colorful old salts had come to an abrupt end.

Duke, Billy, Ken and I gathered in the galley one night in an impromptu wake for our friend. One anecdote led to another as we recalled some of the skipper's humorous adventures. I told the story—which Duke had never heard before—about the night Pete launched himself out of the Boston Whaler. The *Goose* was anchored in Long Beach Harbor at the time (she was due in drydock early the next morning), when the skipper climbed into the Whaler to visit a friend in nearby San Pedro.

It wasn't until after Pete shoved off that he realized he didn't have the boat's ignition key. He drifted about a dozen or so yards off the stern before I heard his shouts for help while I was eating dinner in the galley.

"The key, Bert! Bring me the goddamn key!"

A few minutes later I pulled up next to him in the Dory. Pete grabbed the key from my hand, jammed it in the ignition, hit the throttle and immediately catapulted himself up and out of the boat as the Whaler surged forward. Luckily, the Whaler's motor stalled or it would have taken off for San Pedro on its own. I fished Pete from the drink and rounded up the drifting boat.

But rather than return to the *Goose* for dry clothes, Pete climbed back in the Whaler dripping wet, his shirt and pants clinging to him, soggy deckshoes squishing with each step, and roared off without further delay on his interrupted journey.

When I finished Duke laughed and slapped his hand against the table top. Then he poured tequila all around and offered a toast to the skipper's memory.

Over the years Pete's name would often come up while Duke was visiting in the galley, and we'd start reminiscing about our dead friend. Stories about the skipper were legion and usually hilarious. On more than one occasion, after listening to a favorite Stein anecdote, Duke would shake his head and say, simply and with feeling, "I sure miss ol' Pete."

•

CAPTAIN JACK HEADLEY, A MAN WITH A GOOD SENSE OF HUMOR, A PERPETUALLY tangled clump of brown hair and a first-rate ability to handle both ships and men, took over as the *Wild Goose*'s new skipper. Jack had gone to sea at an early age aboard his father's fishing boat up in the Seattle area, later joining the merchant marine. Like Pete Stein, he was an excellent storyteller, although he lacked Pete's resonant baritone. He had a signature expression for when the going got tough—"Piece of cake," he'd say with utter serenity as all hell was breaking loose around him.

It wasn't long after Jack took command that I lost my heart—and what little sense I had—to a red-haired beauty from Switzerland named Marina.

Marina was Marisa Wayne's governess. Soon we were dating. Duke teased me every time I stopped by the Bayshore house, singing in a loud and very off-key voice, "Ohhhh, how I miss my little Swiss Missssssss . . ."

Still, Duke agreed that Marina was a knockout.

"Man, she's really built," he mused one day as he watched her walk across the patio in a heart-stopping miniskirt.

When Marina unexpectedly flew off to London to study English at a private school (she dreamed of someday being an interpreter at the United Nations), my world collapsed. I thought I'd never see her again. Then a letter arrived telling me she was lonely and missed me, and could I join her in London as soon as possible? I was overjoyed, but also torn between my love for her and my life with Duke aboard the *Wild Goose*. I didn't want to give up one to gain the other.

Love won out, as it usually does. I stayed three wonderful weeks with Marina in London, where we discussed marriage plans. But first it was decided that I should return to Newport, where I could find a job as a carpenter and await her return.

About a month after I arrived home I received a note from my future bride. I tore it open eagerly, having not heard from her since I left London. What the letter said stunned me. My "little Swiss Miss" wrote that she'd met a Frenchman and fallen hopelessly in love. They were to be married!

Suddenly, everything had gone to bloody ruin in my life. I was heartsick. I couldn't

even find a decent job. I finally located work as a "go-fer" and handyman for a local construction firm, although I suspected I was hired only because the owner knew Duke. I'd never been so low. I'd traded a carefree, exciting life aboard the *Wild Goose* for a career as a flunky. I missed the camaraderie of my shipmates and the long, happy hours playing with the Wayne children. And I missed Duke, the best boss I'd ever had. Love not only makes a man blind, it turns him into an idiot.

New skipper, Jack "Piece of Cake" Headley. *Bert Minshall photo*

One night I was sitting in my little mobile home in Costa Mesa, feeling quite defeated, when the phone rang. It was Duke.

I was startled. He began talking as if he'd seen me that afternoon. Actually, it had been almost three months. He told me about an incident that had made the papers several weeks earlier. While he was away filming a movie, thieves had broken into his home and stolen most of his gun collection (although it would later be recovered).

"The bastards cleaned me out," he growled.

He explained that he'd soon be leaving town again to resume location work.

"I was wondering, if you're not busy, how about staying at the house for a couple weeks while I'm gone? Sorta like a house sitter."

I almost shouted into the phone that I'd be happy to watch his house for as long as he wanted.

"That's swell," he said. Then, almost as an afterthought, he added, "By the way, we'll have to see about getting you back aboard the *Goose* this summer."

With that one sentence much of the pain and disappointment of the last few weeks seemed to fade away. I was ecstatic at the thought of rejoining the yacht.

"I'm ready to start tomorrow," I said quickly.

"Well, there's no rush. I'm thinking of taking the boat over to Catalina on Friday. Why don't you come along for the weekend?"

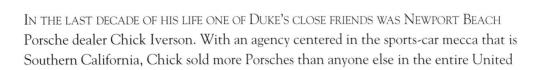

Friday seemed a long time coming. I arrived at the Lido slip well before seven a.m., dressed in my tan uniform. When Jack Headley arrived, he seemed less than thrilled to see me. "I don't know, Bert," he said, shaking his head. "I've already got a pretty good guy for first mate."

Jack was a straight shooter. He told me flat out that he didn't think it was right for me to come waltzing back after leaving the yacht shorthanded and expect to pick up where I'd left off, as if nothing had happened.

"Still, if that's what the Old Man wants . . . " he said, shrugging his shoulders.

I was back aboard ship, but Jack gave me a hard time of it that weekend. He growled at me so often I felt like I was in the lion cage at the zoo. The fellow who had replaced me as first mate understandably resented my return. Not wanting to go back to being a deckhand, he quit the ship entirely. I felt bad about it, but I wasn't going to let anything pry me away from the *Wild Goose* again.

It wasn't until sometime later that I learned how Jack and Duke, after hearing of my sad plight from Ken, conspired to let me stew in my own juices for a few weeks before making a move to get me back aboard ship.

I was steamed at first, but cooled off when I understood their motive. They wanted me to fully appreciate what I'd given up by making it a little rough on me. It worked. By the time Duke called I was one sorry s.o.b. I knew the yacht was where I belonged.

Not long after my return to the *Goose* I was talking with Duke on the patio at his home. It was my first real opportunity to thank him for letting me come back. I told him how much I'd missed the yacht and my association with him and his family. He put a hand on my shoulder.

"It makes a big difference, Bert, when you have a boss who really cares about you."

•

IN THE LAST DECADE OF HIS LIFE ONE OF DUKE'S CLOSE FRIENDS WAS NEWPORT BEACH Porsche dealer Chick Iverson. With an agency centered in the sports-car mecca that is Southern California, Chick sold more Porsches than anyone else in the entire United

BERT'S "LITTLE SWISS MISS," MARINA, ON THE GOOSE'S BOW. *ED FOSTER PHOTO*

States. I'll always remember his first visit aboard the *Wild Goose* around 1970, possibly because he tipped every crew member a hundred dollars.

Chick probably accompanied Duke on more trips aboard the *Goose* than anyone else in Duke's inner circle. The men got along extremely well, even though Chick didn't share one of Duke's consuming passions—cards. But they were a high-spirited— and, at times, hard-drinking—pair of best buddies.

I witnessed only one real falling out between the two men. Although life was casual aboard the *Goose*, Duke usually liked his guests to be showered and more formally dressed for dinner. Nothing fancy, but no shorts, bare feet or T-shirts allowed. "Just because we're on a boat," he once said, "doesn't mean everyone has to look like a bunch of pirates all the time." Weather permitting, dinner would be served on the afterdeck around the large poker table, which would be set with white linen, good silverware, china and lighted candles—and, if possible, a centerpiece of fresh flowers. The ship's steward, uniformed in white and wearing a black bow tie, would serve as combination maître d' and waiter, making sure the meal progressed smoothly.

One night Chick showed up for dinner, as I recall, wearing white tennis shorts. Duke made some comment about Chick's failure to dress properly for dinner. I enjoy wearing shorts myself, and Chick's were neat and clean, but Duke didn't want bare legs at the dinner table. Chick said nothing at the time, but he was obviously irritated— and probably a little embarrassed—by the incident.

For weeks afterward Chick refused all Duke's invitations to sail aboard the yacht. The car dealer was as headstrong as his friend when he felt he'd been wronged. Duke finally persuaded Chick to join him for a trip to Catalina. Each man had missed the other's company. And, when dinnertime arrived, Chick relinquished his God-given right to wear tennis shorts to the table, opting instead for a nice pair of dress slacks. If Duke noticed the fashion surrender (which I'm certain he did), he wisely said nothing about it to Chick.

Duke never shared Chick's understandable passion for Porsches. Although he claimed to have bought the first Corvette sports car sold in California—circa 1955—he had little use for the foreign models.

But I was in love with the fast German road machines. I mentioned to Chick I was thinking about buying a used 911 model, and immediately the dealer told me he'd keep a lookout for one. But after several months passed with no word from Chick, I grew impatient and went out and bought one on my own. The very next day Chick showed up at the Lido slip with big news—he'd found a dream car for me, a 911S in fantastic shape.

"And Bert, you'll never guess who owns it," he went on. "Steve McQueen! He wants to sell it, and I can get it for a good price." Chick thought I'd be thrilled to own the film star's Porsche . . . and he would have been right. There followed an awkward silence as he awaited my reaction. I didn't know any other way to tell him except straight out.

"Hell, Chick. I just bought a 911 yesterday."

Chick stared at me in disbelief.

"You . . . you . . . IDIOT!" he sputtered.

But I was happy with my Porsche, even though it lacked a Hollywood pedigree. My happiness lasted less than a week, cut short when a swerving Ford Mustang clipped the right rear fender of my dream car. The damage was minor, but I was nonetheless crushed. I told Duke about my accident. For several minutes I bitched and moaned about my bad luck. Duke suddenly cut me off with a wave of his hand, a look of irritation on his face.

"Screw the car," he said abruptly. "As long as you're okay, that's all that matters."

I later realized he was right, of course, but it would take a sudden, tragic event to convince me.

●

THE PACIFIC COAST HIGHWAY IS ORANGE COUNTY'S BLOOD ALLEY. IT SEEMS THAT EVERY few days the newspapers report a fatal auto accident somewhere along its twisting, high-speed length. Head-on crashes, motorcycle wrecks and pedestrian fatalities are common. Sometimes, though, a lone vehicle will simply skid off a curve and land in a heap of twisted steel at the bottom of a ravine or beach-front cliff.

Chick Iverson's only son, twenty-year-old Chick Jr., was fatally injured on the Pacific Coast Highway in 1973. He was driving a Jaguar late one stormy night on a wide stretch of highway between Corona Del Mar and Laguna Beach, the famous art colony. According to police, the Jaguar slid off the rain-slick pavement and plunged over a cliff. The driver was still alive when rescue units reached the scene, but he did not survive.

At the time of the accident the *Wild Goose* was anchored more than a thousand miles south at Mazatlán, the city where we'd received the news of Pete Stein's death almost three years earlier. Duke was in Newport attending to business and film matters, although he planned to fly down soon and board the yacht.

Captain Jack Headley learned the tragic news during a routine phone call. The skipper later told me how Duke was "in tears" as he described how young Iverson had clung to life in a Newport Beach hospital, first showing signs of improvement, then suddenly deteriorating. This seesaw between hope and despair was hell on everyone.

Duke, who had been very close to the boy, told Jack it was "the toughest thing I've ever had to go through." Finally, after several agonizing days, Chick Jr. lost his struggle for life. He was buried at Pacific View Memorial Park on a grassy knoll overlooking Pete Stein's grave.

The elder Iverson was devastated. Several weeks later at Chick's Newport agency, the still-grieving father arrived on the lot and noticed a Jaguar among the used sports cars for sale—the same model as the one in which his son had been killed. Chick flew into a rage.

"Get that goddamn thing off my property!" he screamed. "I don't ever want to see one of those here again! Do you hear me? Get it out of here!" A salesman immediately drove the car away.

After the *Goose*'s return to Newport, Aissa Wayne told me a story that made my blood run cold. She said that the night of Chick Jr.'s fatal drive, he'd asked her to go along with him to a party down the coast. (I didn't realize it at the time, but she and the younger Iverson had just started dating.) Aissa was feeling slightly ill and so declined going out on this cold, wet evening. The handsome lad understood. He smiled and said he'd talk to her later.

Then he slipped into his sports car and drove off into the rainy night alone.

A Tough Year

So far, it had been a decade of death for Duke. In 1970 his mother died, as did his younger brother, Bob Morrison. Then, in 1972, his friend and mentor, John Ford, lost a long battle with cancer. And finally the brutal shock of Chick Jr.'s death in 1973. The 1970s were shaping up as a tough time for Duke on the emotional front.

One more personal crisis in his life was coming to a head. His marriage to Pilar was about to fail.

I knew something of Duke's earlier marriages. There was his first wife, Josephine Saenz, whom he had met at Balboa and married after a six-year courtship. By the time they wed, Duke was already in hyper-drive on his film career. Yet he also felt a deep and genuine desire for a family life. Josie fulfilled that desire by giving birth to his first four children—Michael, Toni, Patrick and Melinda. Duke was thrilled to be a father. But, by his own admission, he wasn't around much to play the part because he was too busy playing men of action for the cameras of Hollywood. Duke would be away for weeks, even months, at a time, then return to sweep his children away with a love and attention that was sincere, but also perhaps a little guilt driven. I guess it came down to this, as far as his children were concerned: Duke as a father was either all or nothing.

Increasingly, Josie grew jealous and unforgiving of the time he spent away from home and family making films. On the other side, Duke claimed that his wife's "Old World Ways" and strict Catholic upbringing were hardly the combination to lend spice to their romantic life—four children notwithstanding. He was frustrated with his wife. Whatever the causes and circumstances, both Josie and Duke were unhappy. The marriage gradually fell apart. By 1941 Duke wanted a divorce.

But Josie said no. She didn't believe in divorce. So Duke said the hell with it and went his own way. He saw other women. Finally, after another four years of married limbo, Josie gave in and the couple was divorced in December 1945.

Three weeks later Duke married Esperanza "Chata" Baur, whom he'd been seeing since his break from Josie. As Duke was to joke grimly years later, theirs was a marriage "made in a boxing ring." There were no children, but there were plenty of fights. Chata was spirited and quick-tempered. Together they were like a couple of volcanos matching each other eruption for eruption. Heavy drinking on both sides fueled the fireworks.

In 1953, after eight years of boozy discord, the marriage ended in a spectacular divorce trial in Los Angeles. It was a bloody affair, fought out in the newspapers with all the grace of a cat fight. Duke tried to maintain his dignity through it all, a tough task when your estranged wife is screaming at you from across a crowded courtroom. The proceedings came to a painful end, and with it Duke's second marriage.

When Duke's divorce to Chata became final the following year, he immediately married Pilar, whom he'd met and fallen in love with several years earlier during a

DUKE ROUGHHOUSING WITH MICHAEL (LEFT) AND PATRICK IN THEIR ENCINO HOME. DECEMBER 1942. *SPRINGER/BETTMANN FILM ARCHIVE*

pleasure trip to South America. They were wed on the first of November in Hawaii, where Duke was filming *The Sea Chase* with Lana Turner.

When I met Pilar that first morning off La Paz in 1964, she and Duke had been married almost ten years. I gradually came to realize that she didn't share all her husband's enthusiasm for the yacht. Yet she loved Duke and wanted to please him, so she good-naturedly went along on the cruises. And there were real pleasures for her to enjoy, such as waterskiing and busy days spent exploring the yacht's many interesting ports of call. She liked playing cards and didn't mind keeping Duke company during his numerous fishing trips in the yacht's tenders. She liked the *Wild Goose*, but she still missed the activity and social scene of Newport Beach and nearby Los Angeles.

By the late 1960s, however, the marriage had begun to show signs of real strain. Pilar had grown increasingly dissatisfied with her role as Mrs. John Wayne and the demands it put upon her. It was only natural that part of that dissatisfaction should be turned against her husband's most cherished possession—the *Wild Goose*. Pilar complained of having nothing to do while Duke drank and fished and enjoyed the company of cronies. She said the yacht bored her. That it felt like a floating prison. She soon found excuses to skip voyages, and when she did come along, she didn't always mask her unhappiness.

Several months before they announced their separation, Pilar joined Duke for a trip to Catalina. They went into Avalon one afternoon for a few hours in the British Dory. When they returned to the yacht, they were arguing. I was on the sidedeck and overheard Duke angrily tell her as they walked up the boarding ladder, "Well, you don't have to make it so goddamn obvious to everyone aboard ship that you want a divorce." Pilar, visibly shaken, hurried topside to the master stateroom. Duke stayed in the main salon the

rest of the afternoon, drinking heavily and nursing a smoldering foul mood.

With the wisdom of hindsight I can now see that real trouble may have been brewing between them as early as 1965. It was the time of the *Goose's* remodeling, and Duke and Pilar had driven down from Encino to spend the weekend aboard the ship, which was docked at a shipyard not far from the landmark Crab Cooker restaurant. I was in the galley when I heard angry voices on the afterdeck. It was the first time since joining the ship that I'd heard the couple arguing.

Suddenly, the voices stopped. A moment later Pilar hurried into the galley, plainly very upset.

"Bert, I've decided to leave the yacht and spend the night with the Saftigs," she told me, mentioning close friends of the Waynes' who lived in Newport. "When I'm packed would you please help carry my suitcase?" I told her I would. In truth, I was a little afraid Duke would come storming through the galley door at any moment. Pilar left, and I waited a few minutes before following her topside.

Like a couple eloping in the night, we made our way off the boat and up the dew-covered dock. I lugged Pilar's suitcase as she marched ahead. There was no sign of Duke. A few minutes later we were standing before the red-painted Crab Cooker, with its sign urging passersby to "Eat Lots Of Fish." I phoned for a taxi while Pilar waited outside on one of the benches provided for the restaurant's overflow crowds. It was late, and not many people were around. When the cab arrived, Pilar quietly thanked me for my help. Then the yellow sedan sped down Balboa Boulevard.

When I returned to the yacht I had visions of Duke greeting me with a loaded .45. I didn't want to get caught in the middle of this. But he must have retired to the master stateroom for the night. He was nowhere to be seen.

Neither Duke nor Pilar ever mentioned the incident to me later. The following weekend they were back aboard ship as if nothing had happened. I chalked up the fight to a routine marital spat. But perhaps it was an early sign that their problems ran deeper than anyone—perhaps even they—suspected at the time.

Years later I was eating lunch with Pilar at a restaurant in Los Angeles—she had asked me to play chauffeur for a day of shopping in the city—when she began musing about Duke. Just small talk, really. But then she said something that puzzled me.

"He doesn't know how to treat a woman," she sighed. Her dark eyes seemed far away as she spoke. She rose a little in her chair before looking at me. "Do you know that he's never once taken me out to dinner?"

I couldn't believe that. It didn't seem possible. Certainly she'd had many, many dinners in restaurants with her husband. It wasn't until later that I came to understand what she meant. It was not a literal complaint. It was more symbolic of the subordinate position she had come to believe she held as Duke's wife. She was supposed to support

On November 1, 1954, Pilar Pallete became the third Mrs. John Wayne in a sunset ceremony held in Kona, Hawaii, where Duke had been filming *The Sea Chase*. The film's director, John Farrow (far left), gave the bride away, while Duke's secretary, Mary St. John (second from right), was matron of honor. To the left of St. John is Duke's friend and best man, Francis Brown. District Magistrate Norman Olds (far right) performed the brief ceremony. *AP/Wide World Photos*

quietly her husband's famous persona, which meant being ignored a lot while Duke went about the demanding business of being John Wayne. Pilar was basically a private person. The glare of almost constant public attention irritated her, especially when she wanted her husband to herself. But there always seemed to be a crowd around when they went out—fans or friends or the media or a host of business associates. Armies of strangers monopolized her husband's time. Pilar had started to feel more like an invited guest than a wife. Worse yet, she had begun to feel a distant second to Duke's career. In her eyes, he'd never once taken her out to dinner as a husband would his wife. She had become part of the entourage.

This lack of attention was the same old complaint that had surfaced in Duke's previous marriages—that he poured most of his energies into being John Wayne, and that meant making movies. His being away on location for months was difficult for Pilar. When she did join him on his film trips—as she says he insisted she do—she would be left alone in some hotel room, only to greet an exhausted husband at the end of the day. She eventually refused to go with him on location, which Duke took for disloyalty and lack of interest. The seeds of discontent on both sides were slowly taking root.

Yet Duke loved his wife and did not want to lose her. He worried that the twenty-four-year difference in their ages may have had something to do with Pilar's growing coolness toward him. Deep inside he was afraid that she'd leave him someday for a younger man. His response to that fear sometimes revealed itself in small ways.

For years Duke had not made much effort to hide his baldness in the privacy of his home or aboard the *Wild Goose*. In the early seventies, though, I noticed he was wearing his hairpiece more often, usually when Pilar was around. Considering that Duke was a man of little real vanity, perhaps he did it to appear younger for his wife. It was the only way he could try to turn back the clock and close some of the age gap between them.

At other times, though, he seemed to go out of his way to irritate his wife. His headstrong personality could be difficult for anyone to deal with, especially Pilar, who did not want to play the nag. When Duke started smoking small cigars (probably because his good friend Chick Iverson smoked them), Pilar repeatedly asked him to stop. He

was noncommittal. Pilar couldn't bear to watch him pursue a habit that had already nearly cost him his life. I overheard her say in a moment of frustration that she wouldn't stand by and watch him gradually kill himself in that way. Duke eventually gave up the cigars.

That Duke was genuinely baffled as to how to keep his complex wife happy was underscored by an incident that took place about the time he made *True Grit*. I was riding with him in a rental car on our way to the Scripp's Clinic in La Jolla, near San Diego. Duke was due for a routine checkup at the famous medical facility. Driving was his long-time agent, Jack Gordean.

Jack (who I thought resembled the late Duke of Windsor) had just finished telling a story about a transatlantic trip he'd once taken aboard the Cunard liner *Queen Mary*. In turn, I recalled how I'd seen the legendary ship in Acapulco on her final voyage to Long Beach (where she was later converted into a floating hotel and tourist attraction). I'd talked to some of the Liverpool lads in her crew who boasted—among other things—that the liner's horn could be heard ten miles away. Later, when the great ship was about to depart, I'd persuaded Duke to join me on the *Goose*'s foredeck so we could hear the full glory of this remarkable horn. But the liner had sailed off without so much as a toot to mark her going. Duke had thanked me profusely for a "wonderful experience," claiming that it was a high point of his life. I'd felt double-crossed—and by a British ship, at that! For the rest of the cruise, whenever the *Goose*'s airhorns sounded, Duke would stick his head out the wheelhouse door, cup a hand to his ear, and ask in mock amazement, "Hey, Bert! Is that the *Queen Mary* I hear?"

Jack laughed as I told the story, but Duke remained silent. I asked him if he remembered that visit to Acapulco. "Yeah," was his only comment.

It was several minutes before anyone spoke again. Then Jack asked Duke why Pilar had not come along. That's all it took. Duke launched into a monologue concerning his marriage and its building problems.

A SOMEWHAT APPREHENSIVE
PILAR LOOKS ON AS DUKE IS
GREETED BY A CRUSH OF FANS AND
REPORTERS AT TERMINI TRAIN
STATION IN ROME. ALL TRAIN
TRAFFIC IN AND OUT OF THE ETER-
NAL CITY STOPPED AS RAILROAD
WORKERS LEFT THEIR POSTS TO
CATCH A GLIMPSE OF ONE OF
AMERICA'S MOST FAMOUS
EXPORTS, JOHN WAYNE. DUKE
WAS IN ROME TO MAKE *LEGEND OF
THE LOST* WITH SOPHIA LOREN.
UPI/BETTMANN

"Damn it!" he swore. "I bend over backwards trying to please her, but no matter what I do, she just doesn't seem to care." His voice was heavy with emotion. He looked out at the passing scenery.

"I really don't know what the hell to do," he said, then fell silent once more.

The last time I saw Duke and Pilar together before the separation was at the Bayshore house. I'd come over in the late afternoon to discuss some ship's matter when Duke asked me to stay for dinner. Nothing fancy, he explained. He was sending one of the maids out to pick up some fried chicken. "There's an awfully good chicken joint a couple miles up the Coast Highway," he explained.

A half-hour later I sat down to dinner with Duke, Pilar and Marisa (Ethan and Aissa were visiting friends). A jumble of fried chicken was heaped on a platter on the dining room table. Marisa eagerly dug in. She loved to peel the crispy skin off and drop it into her upturned mouth.

As we ate I noticed that Pilar barely touched her own food. Conversation lagged. She seemed tense and remote. Suddenly, she laid her napkin beside her plate, stood up and, without a word, walked from the room. I looked at Duke. I thought perhaps my presence at dinner had something to do with her sudden disappearance. Duke sensed what I was thinking. "I'm sorry, Bert," he apologized. "Don't worry about it. It's got nothing to do with you."

He never explained what he meant by that. I guess he didn't have to. On November 19, 1973, almost nineteen years to the day after their marriage in Hawaii, Duke and Pilar announced their separation. Although they would never divorce, for all practical purposes the marriage was over. They would never again live together on a steady basis as husband and wife.

Pilar moved with the children into a home in the exclusive Big Canyon area of Newport Beach. She and Duke remained friends after the separation. I never heard either one utter a negative word about the other. Duke saw the children freely. They often stayed with him at the Bayshore house or joined him for cruises aboard the *Goose*. And, while at first I feared that I'd lose touch with the children, Pilar made sure that I was still included in their lives, for which I was grateful.

As with many separations there were attempts at reconciliation. Once Pilar and Marisa flew to London to meet Duke while he was filming *Brannigan*. I saw them off at the airport. Marisa was crying. I asked why, and she said because she didn't want to leave me. She hugged me at the boarding gate. It was as lovely a compliment as I've ever received.

But attempts to patch things up between them ultimately failed. I felt low about them wanting to make it work and not being able to. Yet I was thankful that they refused to allow their children to become casualties of their broken marriage. The love was always there for the youngsters, even if both parents were not.

Some time after the split, I was visiting with Marisa at the Big Canyon home. We were talking about her school as we watched television in the den. I asked her if she had any boyfriends. The great event of Marisa's young life at this time was the discovery of boys. I tried to get her to name names, but she only giggled and said, "Stop being silly, Bert." I then asked her to name her favorite man. I fully expected her to answer Lee Majors, the television actor. I knew she had a crush on the handsome star.

Marisa stopped giggling.

"My dad's my favorite man," she said without hesitation.

DUKE AND PILAR STROLL ALONG A PEACEFUL SHORELINE, UNAWARE OF THE TURBULENT YEARS THAT LAY AHEAD FOR THEIR MARRIAGE. *BERNIE ABRAMSON PHOTO*

Comings and Goings

Despite the hammer blows of 1973, Duke came to accept his separation from Pilar with grace. He was determined to reach for all the good days still within his grasp. As a result, his time aboard the *Wild Goose* became ever more precious to him. There would still be trips to Mexico and the Pacific Northwest and weekends off Catalina. There would be more fish to catch and tequila to drink and jokes to be laughed at. He still had a few more bright years to do as he wished before the twilight set in.

If 1973 was a year of upheaval in Duke's personal life, it also marked the beginning of a two-year period of change aboard the *Wild Goose*. That era began with a wedding.

In the spring Ken married a lovely woman named Teresa in a ceremony held on the yacht. Duke and Pilar attended, although it was clear by then that their own marriage was on rocky ground, as they avoided each other throughout the afternoon. Pilar spent most of the reception in the main salon, while Duke mingled with guests on the afterdeck.

Teresa later told me how Marisa had helped calm her nerves before the ceremony. As the seven-year-old girl helped her adjust her gown and make-up, Teresa admitted she was "scared stiff."

IN STEP WITH THE GOOSE'S CHIEF ENGINEER, KEN MINSHALL. *BERT MINSHALL PHOTO*

"Oh, don't worry," advised Marisa with serene confidence. "Ken's a nice guy."

I was a tad nervous myself. As best man I was worried I might drop the ring or fall flat on my face in front of all those people. Duke and I were standing together near the aft bulkhead. As the minister took his place facing the seated guests, Duke leaned over to whisper in my ear. I expected to hear a few words of moral support.

"Okay, Bert," he hissed as the processional music began. "Start trembling!"

Not long after the wedding Ken announced his plans to retire from the yacht and move up to the Seattle area to skipper his own fishing boat. It had been the best of all worlds having Ken with me aboard ship these past ten years. I hated to think of him leaving. Among other things, Ken was a good man to have in a tight place. A case in point went back to 1964, when Pete Stein suffered his first coronary. At the time the *Goose* was on the ways in Vancouver, Canada, getting her broken bow fixed. Pete flew home to California to rest and recover, and a local skipper was hired to take the yacht down to San Diego, where she'd lay up a few weeks until her slip at Lido Yacht Anchorage in Newport Harbor was available.

The day of our departure, our replacement captain showed up boozed to the gills, a condition in which he would stay for most of the voyage. Ken and I took over navigating, afraid if our soused skipper handled the charts as well as the helm, we might overshoot San Diego and wind up in Ecuador.

Less than five miles from the San Diego breakwater, the bottle finally won its battle for the skipper's heart and mind, not to mention his liver. He was too drunk to get out of his bunk. Ken, as ranking crew member with the most sea experience, took over, guiding the big yacht past Point Loma and into the busy harbor. The moment of truth arrived as Ken eased the *Goose* into her temporary berth, calmly working the helm and gearshifts as if he'd been doing it all his life. In fact, this was his first time at the controls of *any* boat bigger than an outboard runabout. When Duke later heard of Ken's cool prowess at the helm, he was impressed. "Hell, we oughta let Ken run the engines *and* drive the boat." A recovered Pete Stein, arriving aboard ship a couple weeks later, took a somewhat different view of the feat. "Beginner's luck," he muttered.

As engineer, Ken had been responsible for making all the repairs needed to keep the ship's machinery in good working order. Early on Duke noticed how skilled Ken was at fixing things and soon Duke had him doubling as his personal handyman. Whenever an appliance or gadget broke down around the Bayshore house, he'd give it to his driver, Barney Fotheringham, with instructions to "take this over to Ken's Fix-It Shop," for it was in the *Goose*'s well-equipped machine shop that Ken repaired everything from vacuum cleaners to bilge pumps. Duke claimed that if Ken couldn't fix it, it was "pretty well broke."

Ken was driven about keeping the engine room spotless. The giant diesels and generators looked almost antiseptic. And they were in as good shape inside as they were out. Ken rebuilt the mains every eighteen hundred hours of running time, or about every two and a half years, performing at least five major overhauls as chief engineer. It took six hard and dirty weeks to complete the work. Ken's knuckles would be cut and swollen from banging against bolts and sharp metal edges. He'd suffer cramps in his arms that bother him to this day.

The *Goose*'s new engineer, Arnie Moses, didn't think his salary of a thousand

KEN AT THE ORIGINAL NAVY INSTRUMENT PANEL IN THE HEART OF THE *GOOSE*'S ENGINE ROOM, HIS POST AND BATTLE STATION FOR TWELVE YEARS. *BERT MINSHALL PHOTO*

dollars a month required him to perform any major engine work. Almost six years would pass before the diesels received their next overhaul, and then Duke had to hire two freelance mechanics to rebuild the mains. It cost more than thirty thousand dollars, half for labor.

"Good Lord!" Duke exclaimed, flabbergasted by the size of the bill. "I never realized how much money Ken was saving me all those years."

Arnie Moses was about as different from Ken as saltwater is from fresh. He practically lived off black coffee and cigarettes. He spoke in a gruff, sarcastic tone. Duke was amused by his carefully cultivated "I-don't-give-a-damn" attitude. Above all else, Arnie liked to be mysterious. For example, he didn't like having his picture taken. He claimed that certain people were looking for him.

"It might not be too healthy for me if my picture got in the wrong hands," he wheezed, making a smacking sound with his lips and raising his dark, bushy eyebrows.

Arnie claimed he'd once been an informant for the FBI. Something to do with a purloined pension fund and the Teamsters Union. He thought he might be on someone's hit list. One time he asked Duke if he could keep the actor's M-16 rifle aboard ship "just in case." Duke cheerfully agreed, enjoying the engineer's heightened sense of drama. For months Arnie kept the automatic weapon loaded and ready for action by his bunk in his small stateroom located directly over the engine room.

Arnie, though not a handsome man, dated a flashy, stunningly well-built woman who was years younger. He loved to buy her presents. He even bought her a car once. She flew helicopters for a living, and Arnie liked to brag about how she would do anything for a thrill. One day, when she was flying for a TV news station and visibility was poor, her helicopter slammed into the side of a mountain. She was killed instantly. Arnie never completely got over it.

Duke once tried to persuade the engineer to stop smoking. He described his own bout with the Big C. He called cigarettes "cancer sticks." But Arnie wouldn't listen.

In 1983 the engineer died of lung cancer. I had lost touch with him during the years he was sick. We had gone our separate ways. I understand he was quite bitter toward the end. It was a sad finish to an odd and rather tragic life.

•

Arnie Moses was just one of many changes in the ship's crew between 1973 and 1975. Several months before Ken retired, skipper Jack Headley left to start his own marine repair shop. Over the next two years a half-dozen skippers came and went as if propelled through a turnstile. Most left at Duke's invitation.

I remember one skipper who was short in stature but long on aspirations, having decided that the commander of John Wayne's yacht should look more majestic than the current plain tan uniform allowed. His first day he showed up at dockside wearing so much gold braid he looked like a walking deposit from Fort Knox.

When Duke got a look at our sparkling skipper, he whispered to me, "My God, I suppose now *I'll* have to get dressed up whenever I use the boat." He privately complained that his new captain looked like "a reject admiral from the Bolivian Navy."

Duke could have ignored the uniform, but the truth was, he didn't care for the guy. And if he couldn't be friends with his skipper (after all, he owned the boat for fun), then *adios* and good riddance. Our resplendent captain was gone after only a few weeks. He took his uniform with him.

Duke personally balked at firing anyone who worked for him. When it came time for a captain's head to roll, he'd dispatch his two hatchet men, Ernie Saftig and Chick Iverson, to do the dirty work.

Duke was a loyal man, but you had to earn that loyalty. Then it was yours for life. He wouldn't allow anyone to bad-mouth or hassle his friends or employees. Another of Duke's drivers/go-fers, George Coleman, who often accompanied him on movie sets for many years, liked to tell how on location one time the actor stood up for him when some tough guys in the film crew threatened to rough him up. Self-admittedly a little on the obnoxious side, George could raise both hackles and fists. Nonetheless, Duke learned of the threats and confronted those responsible.

"I hear you guys are planning some trouble for George," he told them. "I want you to back off. Now!"

One of the men, however, told Duke that George was an s.o.b. and deserved to get the tar beat out of him. Duke would have none of it. "George may be a sonofabitch, but he's *my* sonofabitch!" The men left the driver alone for the rest of the picture.

We had one short-term skipper whom Duke might also have called an s.o.b., but not with any affection. Instead, this particular captain earned Duke's lasting wrath by ordering all the ship's original navy speaking tubes ripped out. Duke was damn fond of those speaking tubes. I watched as he inspected the pile of bent, broken pipes lying in a twisted heap on the dock. There was a cold, grim look on his face. I stayed in the galley, a safe place, I figured, from which to watch the captain's murder.

"SKIPPER!" Duke bellowed. It was a moment before the captain appeared at the top of the boarding steps.

"Skipper," repeated Duke in a much lower tone but one still edged with homicidal intent. "What's the meaning of this?" He gestured toward the rubble at his feet. "Who gave you permission to tear out those speaking tubes?"

The captain looked surprised. "No one gave me permission to do anything," he said, bristling. "We've got phone intercoms aboard now. We don't need speaking tubes."

Duke was silent as death. Neither man moved. Duke finally spoke.

"All right, that well may be," he said, stressing each word. "But if those tubes aren't put back just like they were, I'm going to personally skin a certain captain alive. You catch my drift?"

I believe the skipper caught it. But it was too late. The speaking tubes were damaged beyond repair. A vain attempt was made to straighten them, but we finally had to cut them up for junk. (I did manage to save the polished brass end caps, one of which I mounted on a teak base for a souvenir.) Not surprisingly, the offending skipper soon left Duke's employ, presumably in search of friendlier waters.

In mid-1975 stability returned to the *Goose* in the person of ex-navy man Jim Maehl. Jim was easy-going and nearly impossible to ruffle, and Duke liked him immediately. With his mustache and round features, he looked like a young Captain Kangaroo. I always thought Jim resembled somebody's favorite uncle.

Inside, however, he was hard as steel. During the Vietnam War he had commanded a river patrol boat in the Mekong Delta. He was a seasoned veteran of the American "brown-water navy." Skippering a large luxury yacht would be a cakewalk by comparison. As Duke said when he learned of Jim's battle experience, at least aboard the *Goose* "nobody would be shooting at him."

A Few Hairy Tales

Over the years Duke developed something of a Dr. Jekyll and Mr. Hyde complex concerning his hairpiece. On one side, there was the time in 1974 when he was invited (challenged might be a better word) to go to Harvard University to accept the "Brass Balls Award" from the Harvard Lampoon. When a student impetuously asked him where he had got his "phony toupee," Duke shot back: "It's not phony—it's real hair." There was a pause. "Of course," he continued, "it's not mine, but it's real!"

Then there was the day he walked into his barbershop in Newport Beach for a trim of his surviving natural growth, threw his toupee in the sink and groused, "I hate that sonofabitch!"

But usually Duke was good-natured about his wig. He liked to slip it on others for a joke. Ken was treated to a toupee test drive one day aboard the *Goose* at Duke's insistence. The hairpiece stayed in place at least three seconds before it slid down onto Ken's forehead. He looked like an early transformation of the Wolfman. Duke and I laughed as he strutted about the afterdeck, the toupee slipping until it nearly covered his eyes. Finally, Duke retrieved the wig and casually tossed it on a couch where it sat like a great, hairy insect.

Clark Powell, one of Duke's business associates and bald to boot, also got an unexpected chance to model the toupee one day at the Bayshore house. Duke looked on, delighted.

"Gee, Clark," he laughed. "If it looks that bad on me, I'm gonna burn the bastard!"

Still, joke as he might, Duke missed his own natural growth. He'd come across obscure remedies that promised to restore his lost follicles. One time he was convinced that a "hair trigger" treatment he was taking could actually grow hair. It was a multistep procedure using shampoos, lotions and vigorous scalp massage. Duke was so excited about the possibilities that he invested money in the treatment's commercial promotion. He tried to get all his bald buddies to try it, including Ken. "Look," he said one day, lowering his head for our inspection. "I'm growing hair! Can't you see it?" All we saw was skin, but we didn't tell Duke that.

As the weeks passed and Duke's head failed to sprout, he spoke less and less of the

A BALD JOHN WAYNE RELAXES WITH ETHAN ON THE GOOSE'S AFTERDECK. AISSA WAYNE PHOTO

amazing new treatment. He no longer claimed he was growing new hair. Eventually, he dropped the subject altogether.

Too much hair and not the lack of it was at the crux of his running feud with Ethan at this time. During the 1970s hair worn below the collar and well over the ears was the badge of young manhood. Duke didn't like it. Like millions of other fathers across the nation, he engaged in a continuing battle with his teenage son over Ethan's flowing locks. Yet he never tried to force Ethan to cut his hair. "It's his choice," he'd say, resigned but not pleased.

ETHAN (REAR) AND FRIEND SPORT THE SHAGGY HAIRSTYLES TYPICAL OF THE 1970S THAT IRKED DUKE AND MILLIONS OF OTHER FATHERS. *BERT MINSHALL PHOTO*

Although he never gave up hounding Ethan to get a haircut, Duke gradually softened his view on the shaggy styles. Perhaps his friendship and admiration for Chick Iverson, Jr., whose brown hair had dropped to his shoulders, played a part in this new understanding. "As long as the kids keep it neat and clean, I guess there's a lot worse they could do," he said.

Neat and clean were words that seldom applied to the Wayne children when it came to picking up after themselves. They were all guilty of overt messiness, possibly as a result of always having servants around to clean up after them.

One afternoon off Catalina, when Marisa was about nine, Duke spotted her clothes strewn about the boatdeck. She had discarded them with careless abandon on her way to change into her bathing suit. Duke boiled over at her sloppiness.

"Dammit," he grumbled, stooping to gather up the loose garments. "I'll teach her to leave her stuff layin' around." Mixed in with Marisa's clothes were those of two of her friends. With a pants leg dangling here and a blouse hanging there, Duke marched to the railing and flung the entire load over the side and into the sea.

It was an ironic display of tidiness considering that you could usually tell Duke's wanderings aboard ship by the debris he left in his wake. It is no mystery where Marisa acquired her haphazard method of changing clothes. Duke would also drop shirts, shoes and pants wherever he happened to remove them. Like father, like daughter.

•

IN THE FALL OF 1974 DUKE FINALLY CURED ME OF A LONG-STANDING HABIT. WHILE sitting by the pool at the Bayshore house, discussing ship's business, I started to call him "Mr. Wayne"—as I had for the past ten years. He stopped me with a wave of his hand.

"Listen, Bert, we've been together a long time," he said, leaning forward and putting a hand on my knee. "At least when we're off the boat, call me Duke."

It was a simple thing, really, but I was touched by the gesture. His conscious show of friendship meant far more to me than if I'd casually fallen into the routine of calling him by his famous nickname.

About this time Duke underwent an operation to raise his badly drooping eyelids.

They sagged so much he was having trouble seeing. After the operation his doctors suggested he wear sunglasses to help reduce the strain from squinting. He refused. As he once told director Henry Hathaway, he wanted his eyes used to bright sunlight because he couldn't wear dark glasses while shooting a scene on location.

His phobia against sunglasses wasn't his only idiosyncrasy. Duke was a pacer, especially aboard ship. He'd walk back and forth as he talked about ship's business or the day's plans, as if impatient to get on with things. He was also lousy at remembering names. As an actor he could memorize pages of dialogue quickly and flawlessly. In everyday life he sometimes couldn't recall the name of a close friend.

California rancher Guy Arnold, whose father was a friend of Duke's, told me how the actor once forgot Maureen O'Hara's name. Duke had known Miss O'Hara for years. He called her one of his truest friends. Yet while relating a story about the actress at a party, his mind went blank. "Oh, hell!" he swore, exasperated. "You know who I mean. The pretty redhead who was in all those movies with me." He was stumped.

Finally, one of his listeners asked in disbelief, "You don't mean Maureen O'Hara?"

"Yeah!" exclaimed Duke in a sudden rush of recognition. "That's her!"

•

ONE CHRISTMAS IN THE EARLY SEVENTIES WHILE THE GOOSE WAS ANCHORED OFF ISLA Grande near Puerto Vallarta, Duke gave Ethan a motorcycle. On the deserted beach the boy tried out his gift, racing up and down the strand, sand shooting out from the spinning wheel in a brown rooster tail. Duke got a kick out of his son's wild ride. Yet as time went by and Ethan's enthusiasm for motorcycles grew, Duke's waned. "I can't even get into the garage anymore because he's got three of his motorcycles in there," he'd complain from a father's viewpoint.

Not long after Ethan started riding, Duke took the boy on a dirtbiking trip to the California desert, about a two-hour drive from Newport Beach. Ken and I went along, having both owned motorcycles for years (respectively, a rugged Bultaco trailbike and an English 650 Triumph set up for off-road racing).

Duke rode with Ethan in air-conditioned comfort in his big Apollo motor coach,

the same one he sometimes used on movie locations, while Ken and I raced ahead on our bikes, picking bugs from our teeth, as the saying goes. Later, as Duke watched Ethan sprinting among the sagebrush on his whining motorcycle, he shook his head.

"Ya know," he said, "if it wasn't for that thing, Ethan would be on horseback right now." To Duke these mechanical mounts of the twentieth century, with their fume-belching and deafening roar, were an assault on nature.

"How can anybody enjoy

DUKE AND "WHAT'S-HER-NAME?" IN *THE QUIET MAN*. DUKE HAD A TOUGH TIME REMEMBERING NAMES, EVEN THAT OF SUCH A CLOSE FRIEND AS ACTRESS MAUREEN O'HARA. *MUSEUM OF MODERN ART/FILM STILLS ARCHIVE*

the outdoors with those noisy contraptions goin' in every direction?" he asked, motioning to other riders racing across the desert landscape.

Before Ethan graduated to motorcycles, Duke bought him a three-wheel Honda ATV which we'd take along on the *Goose*'s cruises, lowering it from the boatdeck with the electric davit at ports of call with likely biking terrain.

RIGHT: ETHAN (REAR), MOTORBIKE AND FRIEND ARE TOWED INTO SHORE IN A SMALL INFLATABLE DINGHY. *BERT MINSHALL PHOTO*

LOWER: DUKE GOES FOR A TRIAL RUN ON ETHAN'S THREE-WHEEL HONDA ATV. *BERT MINSHALL FILM (3)*

One summer while the yacht was docked at Boat Harbor, north of Vancouver, Duke surprised everyone by taking Ethan's ATV for a spin. On a dirt road bordered by pine trees and lush undergrowth, he gamely straddled the tiny vehicle, hit the throttle and took off. Launched might be a more accurate word, as the bike lurched forward, bucking the big balloon front tire off the ground. Duke almost made an unplanned exit—backwards— from the driver's seat. But he held on, risking his hide and his dignity as the contraption settled down onto all three wheels and shot ahead.

It was a sight to remember. Duke, wearing a yellow shirt with a stylish white ascot and yachting cap, weighing probably 240 pounds, his huge frame bolt upright on the seat, looked like a well-groomed block bully making off with a stolen tricycle. But he was having a wonderful time. He sped along the road, once even going after a red sweater that a friend, Herb Broderick, playfully held before him like a matador's cape.

Later that afternoon, Ethan managed to drive his ATV off a thirty-foot cliff. Fortunately, a cluster of young pines cushioned his fall, and both boy and machine escaped with only minor scratches. Duke came running from the *Goose* when he heard of the accident. He was greatly relieved that Ethan was all right. "But damn!" he gasped, trying to catch his breath. "He about gave his old man a heart attack!"

That evening aboard ship, Duke pulled me aside on the boatdeck.

"I want you to keep an eye on Ethan from now on when he rides that thing," he said. "I've had a talk with him about being more careful, but you know how kids are. I'd appreciate it."

I assured him that I'd do all I could, but in truth, short of strapping myself to the ATV's handlebars, I hadn't the slightest idea of how to make good on that promise. Happily, Ethan managed to avoid driving off any more cliffs, and I was able to reap Duke's appreciation for something I had absolutely nothing to do with.

DUKE RIDES SHOTGUN WITH
ETHAN IN THE ACTOR'S APOLLO
MOTOR HOME AS PILAR (IN DARK
GLASSES) RIDES IN BACK WITH
MARISA AND FRIEND. DUKE OFTEN
USED THE BIG VEHICLE ON HIS
MOVIE LOCATIONS. *PHIL STERN
PHOTO*

Once Again North

British Columbia continued to be one of Duke's favorite cruising spots. I believe he probably enjoyed these trips even more than those to Mexico. Meeting up with old friends was a special treat. Max Wyman would often rendezvous with the *Goose* aboard his *Silverado*. We'd "raft" the two boats together, tying them gunwale to gunwale, so all Duke and Max had to do to visit was step from deck to deck.

There were other friends who came visiting, such as Ernest Gann, author of *The High and the Mighty*. Gann lived on a three-hundred-acre ranch near Friday Harbor on

San Juan Island. The writer was an accomplished artist and during his shipboard stays tried to teach Duke and the children how to sketch. Duke never showed much promise as a budding artist, but he diligently followed his friend's instructions, a pencil cradled in his big hand, intent on getting the lines and shading right.

One summer while the *Goose* was docked at Victoria, a lovely Canadian city located on Vancouver Island, Duke met up with comedian Bob Hope and his wife, Dolores, who had chartered the 140-foot *Principia* for several weeks of cruising and fishing. It was the height of the summer boating season, and docking space was full up, so the *Principia* had to tie up to the *Goose*'s starboard side.

Early the next morning, on their way ashore, the Hopes stopped briefly to chat with Duke on the *Goose*'s boatdeck. I joined them to take a few snapshots.

Accompanying the Hopes was the couple's small white poodle. As Dolores Hope held its leash, the dog sniffed suspiciously at Duke's leg. The scene was set for one of the more infamous acts ever committed aboard the *Wild Goose*. The dog apparently mistook the figure towering over him for a behemoth fireplug. It was a moment before Duke realized that he was being peed on by a poodle. He jerked his foot away, but not before his pant leg was soaked.

Duke and Bob looked at each other. Then the two men exploded in laughter.

"My God, Bob!" roared Duke. "I sure hope that wasn't anything personal!"

I thought the comedian was going to collapse. Dolores looked embarrassed, but also joined in the laughter. The poodle, however, continued to eye Duke's shin in a dangerous manner.

THE 126-FOOT *SILVERADO*, FOR SEVERAL YEARS DURING THE 1970S THE WORLD'S LARGEST FIBERGLASS-HULLED YACHT. BUILT BY SEATTLE LUMBER MAGNATE MAX WYMAN, FORMER OWNER OF THE *WILD GOOSE*. *BERT MINSHALL PHOTO*

RIGHT: GETTING A DRAWING LESSON FROM ERNEST GANN, AUTHOR OF *THE HIGH AND THE MIGHTY*, AT GANN'S BRITISH COLUMBIA RANCH.

LOWER: BERT AND BOB HOPE ON THE *GOOSE'S* BOATDECK WHILE THE YACHT WAS DOCKED IN VICTORIA, ON CANADA'S VANCOUVER ISLAND. *BERT MINSHALL PHOTOS (2)*

After the Hopes left and Duke had changed into a dry pair of pants, he joined me in the galley. He was still laughing about "that damn dog!" He told me this was not the first time he'd been used as a toilet, although it was the first by a canine. He said he was eating dinner one evening with friends at the Balboa Bay Club in Newport Beach—one of his favorite hang-outs—when he excused himself to go to the restroom. Once inside he walked to the nearest available urinal.

"Well, there was this guy standin' at the next one," explained Duke, a crooked grin on his face. "After a few seconds he sorta turns his head and looks over, just curious, I guess, to see who's beside him. All of a sudden, his eyes get real big, and he whirls around and says, 'Jeezus Chrrrist! It's John Wayne!' "

Duke laughed, shaking his head.

"Bert, that guy stood there and pissed all over my leg!"

•

OUR TRIPS NORTH WERE NOT COMPLETE WITHOUT AT LEAST ONE GIFT-BUYING BLITZ BY Duke in Victoria. Over the years he spent thousands of dollars here on presents for his friends and family.

Duke always carried a wad of cash on him during trips ashore—whether it was in Catalina, Mexico or Canada—in case something caught his eye. Something usually did. He'd return to the yacht loaded with gifts and souvenirs.

Pilar had warned him years earlier that he'd spoil the children with his gift buying, but he derived such vast satisfaction from playing year-round Santa Claus that she could never bring herself to put a damper on his fun.

One summer off Catalina Duke bought Ethan an expensive toy boat that he'd come across in a shop in Avalon. It was a sleek little craft that could sail under its own power. Ethan was a resourceful child, and by the time the *Goose* returned to Newport he'd managed to trash the toy. It looked like a miniature version of the wreck of the *Hesperus*.

The contest was on. On our next trip to Catalina Duke bought Ethan another

boat. History repeated itself as the boy turned the handsome vessel into a floating disaster.

All told, Duke probably bought four or five boats for Ethan during the course of the summer, only to have the boy destroy one after the other. Duke was greatly amused by his five-year-old son's inventive destructiveness.

"Ya know, the manufacturer of those boats oughtta hire Ethan to field test all his toys," he mused one day on the afterdeck, as he inspected the shattered remains of one of the ill-fated fleet. "If they survive more than two days with the boy, then, by God, they're built to last!"

It wasn't long after Bob Hope's poodle christened his pants leg that Duke purchased for Aissa in Victoria a beautiful green suede coat lined with black Persian lamb's wool. But when the coat was later delivered to the boat, Duke detected a peculiar odor he hadn't noticed at the shop. No one could identify the smell, but it seemed to be getting stronger by the minute. Duke picked up the reeking garment and held it before him like a dead animal.

"Christ Almighty!" he exclaimed, wrinkling his nose. "They must've cured the leather with camel pee."

One of the wits in the crew suggested that perhaps the Hopes' poodle had visited the shop earlier. We tried everything we could think of to rid the coat of its stench. We left it out in the sun and fresh air for several days. We took it to a dry cleaner. Duke even tried dousing it with Aissa's perfume to mask the scent. Nothing worked.

Duke threatened to take the coat back to where he'd bought it, but he never did. I think it ended up in a self-service storage unit in Costa Mesa, stashed among a treasure trove of John Wayne memorabilia that included prints of many of the actor's films, old costumes, furniture and other personal belongings.

•

ALL WAS NOT FUN AND GAMES DURING OUR LATER NORTHERN CRUISES. WHEN DUKE made McQ in Seattle in 1973, he used the Goose as his dressing room and living quarters. Of course, things were not going well in his marriage at the time. Add to this the pressures of filming, and Duke was working on a short fuse.

In the movie, Duke's character drives a high-powered Pontiac Trans Am. Duke liked the car's muscle but not the cramped fit. He complained that he constantly banged his head against the roof.

"I'm gonna beat my brains out before the end of the picture," he told me one day after work. He also had difficulty entering and exiting the vehicle with any semblance of grace. He finally asked the propmen to install a swivel seat as low as possible on the driver's side. He thought this would help him maneuver in and out, plus solve his headroom problem.

Studio crews went to work on the car. When the modifications were finished the vehicle was brought over to the Seattle Yacht Club—where the Goose was berthed at Max Wyman's private dock—for the actor's approval.

Knowing my addiction to fast cars, Duke asked me along to inspect the Trans Am as he tried out the swivel seat. The trial run did not go well. He had trouble making the seat work, and his head still bumped the roof. He was inside the car less than a minute when the door opened and he scrambled back out. He turned angrily to one of the film crew.

"Goddamnit, it's just as bad as before. You guys fucked up. Put it back the way it was." Then he marched back to the yacht, leaving me with a group of stunned propmen.

Another explosion took place after Duke toured a local antique shop looking for furniture for the boat. He saw a few things he liked and asked that they be delivered to the yacht club. A day or so later, when a truck arrived from the store, Duke and I strolled up the dock to supervise the unloading. But when the driver opened the truck's rear door and Duke glanced inside, his face flushed.

"What the hell's the matter with you?" he demanded. He waved his arm at the contents of the truck. "That's not what I wanted. Take that crap back."

Duke left the driver standing wide-eyed as he strode away. After a long, awkward moment, I asked the shaken driver what was going on. He said he didn't know. He claimed the items he brought were the ones his boss told him Duke had ordered.

And yet, such shows of temper were relatively rare. Duke's innate good humor and friendliness more often than not brought out his better side, especially during his encounters with fans. It usually didn't take long for word of his arrival to spread through an area. Soon, a crowd of admirers would gather at dockside or along the shore. I doubt if a human being ever lived his life in a fishbowl quite as gracefully as Duke did. Perhaps the affection he received from his fans made that fishbowl seem more a blessing to him than a curse.

Even when Duke wasn't aboard, the *Goose* was something of a celebrity in her own right, easily recognized all along the North American Pacific coast. Crowds often turned out simply to get a look at the yacht during her visits.

(The *Goose* was not the only converted minesweeper of her class that was well known to the public. *Calypso*, the research vessel of famed oceanologist and explorer Jacques Cousteau was a sister ship of the *Goose*. Both vessels were built in the same

A TENDER MOMENT BETWEEN PILAR AND DUKE, IN SPITE OF THE BUILDING TENSIONS IN THEIR MARRIAGE. *GLOBE PHOTOS*

Seattle shipyard by the Ballard Marine Railway Company during World War II, and both saw service during that war, although the *Calypso* was sold to the British Navy and ended up as a patrol boat off Gibraltar, while the *Goose* was commissioned as a U.S. minesweeper for duty in the Aleutian Islands off Alaska. While the *Goose* may have been known to thousands along the Pacific seaboard, the *Calypso* was a bona fide star to millions due to Cousteau's many TV specials and because of her role as the seagoing heroine of a popular song, the *Calypso* hymn, by singer John Denver.)

Not everyone, however, was in love with Duke—or Americans, for that matter—during our trips north.

In 1971, while the yacht was moored at her usual slip in front of the Empress Hotel in Victoria, the United States was scheduled to conduct an underground atomic test at Amchitka in the Aleutian Islands. Although Amchitka was more than 1,700 miles from the Canadian border, the upcoming test had raised a storm of controversy in that country. Predictions were widespread that the explosion would trigger earthquakes and tidal waves.

One afternoon some Canadian journalists came aboard to interview Duke. Unexpectedly, one of them asked him his opinion about the Amchitka test. He briefly told the reporters that what America did in her own country did not concern the Canadian government, and vice versa. They had asked his opinion and he'd given it.

When the story came out, it sounded as if John Wayne was telling the entire country of Canada to go collectively shove it. Canadian editorialists condemned him. Duke thought the reporting had been slanted, but he felt it best to let the incident blow over without further comment.

I didn't detect any resentment or hostility among the crowds of Canadians who continued coming to the yacht's berth. Many of the visitors I talked to felt the controversy surrounding the interview was much ado about nothing.

Several days after the interview hit the media, I noticed a dour-looking young man approaching the yacht's stern. Suddenly, he leaned out and spit on the *Goose*'s varnished transom. By the time I made my way onto the dock, the expectorating avenger was already fast-footing it through a crowd of Canadian tourists. I gave chase, but he disappeared among the rows of cars in the hotel's parking lot. I hiked back, furious over losing him.

It happened so quickly that no one in the crowd had thought to grab the fellow as he darted past them. When people realized what he'd done, a chorus of boos broke forth. People gathered around me and apologized for his behavior. They were outraged at such crudeness.

Duke was away from the yacht at the time. I never told him about the incident. The kind reaction of the crowd dispelled much of my anger. I walked back to the yacht and hosed off the transom, then wiped it clean. Nonetheless, I admit that I'd rather have buffed it out using the skinned hide of our young friend.

EARLY MORNING IN NORTHERN
WATERS. *Bert Minshall photo*

Of Time and Charters

As his children grew older Duke had hoped their enthusiasm for the yacht would continue undiminished. To him the children had been the heart of his shipboard life. Although he understood they were becoming independent, with interests of their own, he didn't much like it when those interests led them away from the *Wild Goose*. Time was flying by, he knew, and gradually taking his children with it.

Time had indeed flown. Aissa, the seven-year-old girl I'd awkwardly shaken hands with that first day off La Paz was now attending USC. In a few more years she would be married and raising a family of her own.

But it was Marisa and Ethan who really made the *Goose's* first mate feel the passage of the years. I could commiserate with Duke and Pilar on the bittersweet joys of watching their children grow up. I wanted the happy days I'd spent with the children aboard the *Wild Goose* to keep right on going. I wanted an endless summer of youth. But somehow every bloody one of us just kept getting older.

•

When Ethan was about fourteen Duke bought him a twenty-two-foot day cruiser in which to putter around Newport Bay. The inboard powerboat was docked not far from the *Goose*. It had sat for some time, and water had got into the fuel tank. I'd have to change out the gas for new before we could take the boat on a test run.

As it turned out, I did more than siphon out the contaminated gas. I nearly blew the boat and myself to kingdom come. I was using a portable pump from the *Goose* to empty the tank into a five-gallon can when gas started overflowing onto the dock. I didn't want to let go of the siphon hose, so I gave a quick yank on the pump's extension cord, thinking I could pull it from its outlet at the head of the dock. Instead, the cord popped free from the pump. Suddenly, there was a loud whoosh and I was standing knee-deep in flames. A spark must have ignited the gas that had spilled. Having no intention of being the main dish at a bayside barbecue, I dove into the water.

The quick dousing saved me. But when I looked back at the dock I saw a wall of flame shooting skyward. My horrifying fear was that the flames would spread through the anchorage. As I swam for a safe place to pull myself out I saw Ethan, who'd been back at the *Goose* retrieving another fuel can, running along the dock, dragging the berth's freshwater hose behind him. The fast-acting lad washed the burning gasoline off the dock into the water. It floated on the surface a moment, a scum of flame, before going out.

It was a close call. I was proud of how Ethan had handled the emergency. If I needed any proof that he was growing up to be a responsible young man, this was it. As for me, I suffered only a few minor burns on my legs. It was something of a miracle that the flames had not ignited the fuel can. It could have blown us to Catalina.

A few days later, I asked Ethan what his dad had said when he heard about the fiery mishap. Ethan shrugged his shoulders.

"He called you a dumb shit," said the boy.

Sometimes, I thought, Ethan could be a tad *too* honest.

About the time I nearly burned down Newport Beach, Pilar suggested that I take up tennis so I could play with Ethan and Marisa. (With Pilar's enthusiastic backing, Duke had become half-owner of the private John Wayne Tennis Club near the New-porter Inn—although I don't know if Duke ever swung a tennis racket in his life.)

Tennis turned out to be one of the few sports I ever played with the children that was not water-oriented. Marisa, like her mother, loved the game. She got so good that she could consistently beat Ethan. He didn't like it much. I know how he felt. It was disconcerting how the young girl could pound my male ego into the court with a flurry of volleys, backhands and screaming line shots.

Duke tried not to show favorites among his children, but he couldn't help playing the role of doting father with young Marisa. I'm sure he knew it would be his last opportunity to do so.

I recall one trip to Acapulco when I came across Duke and Marisa talking on the boatdeck. I picked up my movie camera and started filming. Unexpectedly, Duke leaned down and kissed Marisa on the forehead. The girl giggled as he tried to kiss her again, this time on the bridge of the nose. As I continued filming he cradled his daughter's head against his massive chest. "Well, aren't we a silly pair," he said, then reached down and gave her nose a gentle tweak.

•

MARISA TAKES THE HELM. *BERT MINSHALL PHOTO*

I RECEIVED A NUMBER OF GIFTS FROM DUKE OVER THE YEARS. USUALLY AT CHRISTMAS HE gave me something I could use aboard ship. One year he presented me with an expensive jacket with the ship's insignia—a pair of crossed pennants, one depicting a flying goose in silhouette, the other the official ensign of the Newport Harbor Yacht Club, of which Duke was a member. Above the pennants the words *Wild Goose* were sewn in script. But there were other times when the gift giving was unexpected.

Sam Lluchese was Duke's bootmaker for many years. The small, dark-haired Italian craftsman made high Western fashion out of the skin of snakes, alligators, lizards, sharks, even certain types of exotic fish. Duke usually stayed with traditional cowhide.

Duke was one of Sam's few clients who rated a house call for a private fitting. I understand Sam once refused to make a pair of boots for Cher because the singer-actress couldn't visit his shop in San Antonio, Texas, to be measured. She offered to pay Sam's way to come out to Los Angeles to fit her. The feisty bootmaker said no, even though the boots she was interested in cost $2,500.

Every couple of years Duke had Sam make him several new pairs of boots. Although Duke was big as a building, he wore only about a size ten. His feet were almost delicate compared with the rest of him.

During one of these in-home fitting sessions Duke asked if I'd like Sam to make me a pair of boots. I couldn't see myself going in debt for something I might never wear.

"Hell, Duke," I told him. "They look pretty expensive."

"Don't worry about that. It's my treat. Just pick out a style you like. Sam'll fit you."

I picked out a simple design, one I hoped didn't cost too much. Sam didn't believe in putting prices in his albums.

Duke was in a boot-giving mood. Before I left he also had Sam measure his secretary, Pat Stacy, and his driver, Barney Fotheringham, as well as a visiting business partner for footwear.

Some months later my custom boots arrived from Texas. I tried them on, and they fit perfectly. Pat Stacy later let me peek at the bill. Those "simple" boots cost Duke three hundred dollars—and this was in 1976. All told, he gave away more than two thousand dollars in footwear that day.

It was extravagant, of course, and that was a big part of Duke's personality. He made a lot of money and he spent it—sometimes unknowingly. Duke used to claim that a couple of former business managers nearly managed him into the poorhouse. He said one manager cost him seventeen million dollars. It's been reported that over the years Duke was involved in everything from a now infamous fleet of Panamanian shrimp boats to a comic-book-publishing company.

There's no doubt that the *Wild Goose* was a major cash drain. Almost from the beginning Duke had made the yacht available for charter on a limited basis to help defray the ever-rising cost of running the boat, which by the mid-seventies topped $150,000 a year. The bare-boat charter fee ran a thousand dollars a day. To this were added fuel costs, crew wages, insurance, cleaning fees, food, booze and so forth. The average daily cost of chartering the vessel could easily reach two thousand dollars or more.

Many of these charters over the years were to film companies. Television series such as the old spy thriller *The Man from U.N.C.L.E.* and the cop show *Felony Squad*

WITH SAN ANTONIO BOOTMAKER SAM LLUCHESE. DUKE IS SPORTING A MUSTACHE AND GOATEE FOR HIS UPCOMING ROLE IN *THE SHOOTIST*. *BERT MINSHALL PHOTO*

ETHAN GETS A CLOSE-UP LOOK AT
SAM LLUCHESE'S HANDIWORK.
JOHN R. HAMILTON PHOTO

AISSA (LEFT) WITH LYNDA BIRD
JOHNSON, DAUGHTER OF THEN
PRESIDENT LYNDON B. JOHNSON,
AND FRANCESCA, DAUGHTER OF
WAYNE'S FRIEND ACTRESS MERLE
OBERON. OFF ACAPULCO. *AISSA
WAYNE PHOTO*

either shot scenes aboard or used the yacht for background. She appeared in movies such as *The President's Analyst*, starring James Coburn, and writer Sidney Sheldon's *The Other Side of Midnight*.

In addition to celebrities such as Dean Martin, Hugh O'Brien, Tom Jones and Jackie Gleason, others who spent time aboard—as guests or due to film work or their own private charters—included Frankie Avalon; George Raft; Howard Duff; Linda Bird Johnson and her then boyfriend, George Hamilton; John Derek and *his* then wife, Linda Evans (Derek would later wed the spectacular Bo); Princess Grace (Kelly) of Monaco; David Niven; William Holden; Henry Ford II; Aristotle Onassis (before Jackie); director Otto Preminger, and Carol Channing (who brought along a number of offbeat gourmet delicacies, including a jar of pickled frogs' legs). One of my personal favorites was the time in 1975 when entertainer Sammy Davis, Jr., spent a week aboard the yacht cruising off Catalina.

Friendly, funny and casually profane, Sammy was a great admirer of Duke's. Sammy enjoyed a reputation as a legendary partymaker, but Duke wasn't worried that he might destroy the yacht.

"You guys let Sammy do whatever he wants to while aboard," he instructed us a few days before the charter.

Those first days at Catalina Sammy spent by himself just relaxing and reading.

Later in the week he was joined by his wife and some friends who flew to the island by seaplane.

The entertainer brought with him a portable video machine (rare in those days) along with a number of taped movies, including a few of Duke's, which he played over the main salon's television. There were also some X-rated titles. Sammy gave the crew permission to watch his shipboard film library in our offtime. The X-rated fare, I'm afraid, received the heaviest use.

One evening Sammy wandered into the main salon and caught several crew members—including the first mate—entranced by that fine cinematic classic *Deep Throat*. The gawking sailors ignored him as he walked over to the bar.

"You bastards," he grinned, before turning to mix himself his usual gin and Coke.

Billy Sweatt and Sammy hit it off well. As the two small men stood next to each other, the singer joked that they looked like a pair of salt and pepper shakers. Billy had some difficulty adjusting to the entertainer's shipboard hours. Sammy would sleep from late afternoon through the evening, awaken around midnight, and then ask the cook to prepare him a steak sandwich. He would stay up through the rest of the night and well into the following afternoon.

Only once did Sammy lose his good humor during the voyage. One evening, television reception kept fading while the yacht was anchored on the windward side of the island. Sammy, who was trying to watch the news, thought the TV was broken. I tried to explain that the island itself was blocking the signal coming in from Los Angeles, but he was quite upset and demanded that I get someone "over here" immediately to fix the set.

"I don't care what it costs," he said, pulling from his pocket a wad of bills the size of a baseball. "I've got it on me."

It was only a momentary squall in what was otherwise a calm trip. On our way back to Newport Beach he strolled into the wheelhouse and struck up a conversation with the *Goose*'s current captain. Jim Maehl had not yet joined the yacht.

SAMMY DAVIS, JR., AND BILLY SWEATT DURING THE ENTERTAINER'S CATALINA CHARTER. BERT MINSHALL PHOTO

"Here, Sammy," said the skipper, motioning to the helm. "Do you want to steer the boat?"

Sammy looked at him in mock horror.

"Hell no! Do I ask you to sing *Candy Man*?"—a reference to his biggest song hit.

Duke met us at the slip as we pulled in that last day. He towered over Sammy as he greeted him warmly in the main salon. Duke put a huge arm around the small man's shoulders.

"How'd it go, Sammy?" he asked.

"Wonderful, Duke," replied the entertainer, nearly disappearing in Duke's massive hug. "Just wonderful!"

Change of Command

We had just finished lunch in the galley when we heard the roar of the twin-engine Piper Navaho as it sped in low over the sun-scorched fishing village of Turtle Bay, located about halfway down the Baja coast. The red-and-white plane circled the *Wild Goose*, dipped its wings in greeting, then headed off for a dirt landing strip outside of town we had grandly dubbed Turtle Bay International Airport.

The Piper belonged to Chick Iverson, and this afternoon Duke and a few friends had flown in it from Orange County to keep a rendezvous with the *Goose*. (Duke had owned a number of aircraft over the years—including a small jet and a couple of helicopters—but by the mid-1970s, when he needed a small plane, Chick usually volunteered his speedy craft.)

After a quick trip ashore in the British Dory and a bouncing ride over dirt roads in the town's only taxi cab, I arrived at the landing strip, where Duke was passing out the last doughnuts from a large box he'd brought for snacks on the trip down. Duke loved doughnuts, especially the cut-out holes. Back in Newport Beach he liked to visit a little joint, not far from the old Balboa Fun Zone, that sold the sugar-coated holes by the bagful.

I knew Duke was coming off a bout of flu, but his appearance this afternoon alarmed me. The illness had left his face pale and slightly puffy. His eyes seemed flat and the lids swollen. He'd lost weight. His shirt collar hung about his neck. His movements were deliberate, as if he wasn't quite sure of his balance. When he spoke, his voice sounded raspy.

As we piled into the taxi for the short ride into town, I tried to put my concern out of mind. I reasoned that anyone would look wrung out coming off the flu. And yet there was something more to it than that.

The first few days aboard ship were low-key, as Duke rested and relaxed in the warm sun. Just being on the *Wild Goose* again seemed to work a transformation in him. As the days passed, Billy's good cooking helped him gain back the weight he'd lost. The sun put the color back in his face. He was rapidly regaining his vigor.

My earlier concern fell away as Duke became his old self again. He was fishing and drinking with renewed gusto. I was impressed

WITH JIMMY STEWART, WHO PLAYED A FRONTIER DOCTOR IN DUKE'S LAST FILM, *THE SHOOTIST*. MUSEUM OF MODERN ART/FILM STILLS ARCHIVE with his recuperative powers. I remember thinking that he had the constitution of an ox.

In the past, when cruising aboard the *Goose*, if Duke had a movie coming up, he'd often bring along the script to study in his spare moments. On this particular trip, sitting on his dresser in the master stateroom was the script of a film he was due to start shooting on his return to California. The title on its cover page said *The Shootist*.

At the time I didn't know there was a scene in that script where Duke's character visits a frontier doctor and finds out he has cancer. He's surprised and tells the doctor that he's always been as strong as an ox.

Yes, says the doctor. But even an ox dies.

•

BY 1977 IT WAS OBVIOUS THAT DUKE'S HEALTH was failing. He no longer could stand the extended rigors of moviemaking. Although he had a number of investments, including a sprawling cattle ranch in Arizona, he still needed a substantial cash flow to survive. For income he turned to making television commercials, first for a pain remedy, then for Great Western Savings, based in Los Angeles.

DUKE STEADIES A PROTEIN DRINK ON THE CONSOLE OF THE BRITISH DORY ON HIS WAY INTO SHORE TO FILM A TELEVISION COMMERCIAL. HE CLAIMED THAT THE DRINK GAVE HIM ENERGY BUT TASTED "LIKE HELL." *BERT MINSHALL PHOTO*

Once Duke had decided to do the commercials he insisted they be first-rate. He used the best film crews, the best scripts and his own professionalism to make television spots that had the appeal of mini-movies. They would eventually win awards for being among the best on TV. Great Western Savings was ecstatic—by the end of 1978 the banking firm claimed that Duke's commercials had helped bring in a quarter *billion* dollars in new revenue. (In fact, the spots proved so popular with viewers that some time after Duke's death they were rerun for several weeks as a tribute.)

Duke filmed several commercials in the Seattle area, using the *Wild Goose* as a base of operations. One morning I accompanied him in the Dory on his way into shore to begin the day's shooting. The roar of the outboard motor broke the morning calm as we raced across the inlet. Behind us the *Goose* swung at anchor in the still water. Duke was dressed in his classic Western garb—sweat-stained Stetson, neckerchief, leather vest, holster, boots and spurs. In the holster was his favorite Colt "Peacemaker" .45, a gun he'd used in many of his films.

Duke looked great. Still, there was perhaps no better sign of his lagging strength these days than the protein drink he sipped as we rode into shore. He said it was "good for my energy." Between swallows he steadied his glass on the Dory's center console.

"Tastes like hell, though," he added.

When we made shore Duke turned to me before climbing into a car for the ride to his film location.

"Try to hold down any mutinies until I get back," he said, grinning. Then he swept his arm toward the *Wild Goose* across the water.

"Well, she's all yours . . . *Captain* Minshall."

•

I'D NEVER SERIOUSLY CONSIDERED BUCKING FOR COMMAND OF THE *WILD GOOSE*. BUT then Jim Maehl announced he was leaving the yacht to take the helm of another boat, the 115-foot *Serendipity*, which was due to leave Newport for an extended voyage in the Mediterranean. He also told me he was putting in the word with Duke that I should be the *Goose*'s next skipper. I wished I'd been as sure about this as he seemed to be. I was happy as first mate. I knew my duties and performed them as well as I could. I suppose the thought of being captain intimidated me.

Apparently, it also intimidated Duke when he first heard about it. He wasn't sure I had the right skills for the job. But unknown to him, Jim had been tutoring me the past three months in the nuances of handling the 287-ton yacht, patiently teaching me what combinations of throttle and helm to use to maneuver and compensate for wind and current. Jim felt I'd done well, even though I was unaware that he'd been grooming me to take command. He told Duke I would be a fine skipper—an act of faith on Jim's part for which I'm grateful to this day. Duke, still not used to the idea, nonetheless said he'd give me a shot.

My tryout cruise as skipper nearly came to grief when the yacht's big Cleveland GMC diesels mysteriously overheated and started blowing steam to beat Old Faithful. We were on a weekend cruise to Catalina. Duke, in what I took to be a show of confidence, had bravely brought along Ethan and Marisa on Captain Minshall's first solo voyage.

He must have been having second thoughts as the *Goose* wallowed in the swells, dead in the water, and her novice

DUKE WITH SKIPPER JIM MAEHL, JIM'S FATHER MURRAY MAEHL AND ERNIE SAFTIG. *BERT MINSHALL PHOTO*

skipper went sprinting past him and down into the engine room. Arnie Moses wasn't aboard this trip, having taken off a few days earlier on a long-planned vacation. Filling in was Jim Maehl's father, Murray, a fine seaman with a working knowledge of the old navy engines, but who at this moment was barely visible through the clouds of hot vapor. He was working frantically on a row of valves, a large wrench in his hands.

"Don't know what happened, Bert," he shouted above the noise when he saw me. "They just started blowin' steam all of a sudden. They're overheated, but I don't know why. I sure hope they aren't fried."

This was really what I wanted to hear. I told Murray to do the best he could and climbed the engine-room ladder to the afterdeck. Duke was waiting for me as I emerged from the companionway.

"What's goin' on?" he asked, stepping back.

"I don't know," I said. An honest answer, but hardly one to instill confidence. Duke looked at me suspiciously. I explained what Murray had told me.

"Well, you're the captain," he said. "It's your ballgame, Bert."

I was rather wishing that it *wasn't* my ballgame, but I knew I'd have to get some help for Murray. I put in a call over the ship's radio to a marine diesel shop in Newport, asking that a couple of mechanics be dispatched by small boat to lend us a hand (we were only about three miles off the breakwater). But when I told Murray what I'd done, he looked at me as if I'd just hit him in the head with a tire iron.

"Aw, hell," he groaned. "You didn't need to do that. I just found the problem."

Apparently, Murray had overlooked opening the main sea valves to the engines. They'd overheated because there was no cooling water circulating. Murray was extremely embarrassed, but I told him to forget it. Not many men would have had the guts to step cold into a World War II-vintage engine room and take over. It was a simple mistake. Fortunately, the engines fired up with no discernible damage, although I told Murray that we'd better let the two mechanics en route take a look at them, just to be on the safe side.

Of course, while all this was going on, Duke was pacing the afterdeck wearing his "Is-Bert-fit-for-command?" look. But he still said nothing as I hurried by.

The mechanics soon arrived, the mains were pronounced healthy, and the *Goose* was once again under way for Catalina. Duke couldn't have asked for a more timely test of Bert Minshall under pressure. I must have come through it all right. The rest of the trip went smoothly. But I'd received a vivid education on the burdens of being skipper.

•

I OFFICIALLY ASSUMED COMMAND OF THE *WILD GOOSE* IN SEATTLE DURING THE SUMMER of 1977 on our annual cruise to the Pacific Northwest. Jim had taken the yacht on the first leg of the journey. He shook hands and wished me luck before leaving to fly back to Newport and his new ship.

I'd come a long way in time and circumstance since I first set foot on the *Goose* in Barcelona as a green deckhand. I was now forty-three, not a brash thirty. I'd sailed close to sixty thousand sea miles. I'd watched and helped the Wayne children grow up. And John Wayne, at one time just a face on a movie screen to me, was now my friend. It was humbling to think how lucky I was. It'd all been so bloody much fun.

I loved the Pacific Northwest best of all the places I'd voyaged with Duke. Now, as skipper, I was no longer so happy-go-lucky as I'd once been about taking in the sights. I worried about every unexplained ripple in the water's surface, thinking perhaps it marked the location of a submerged log or shoal. I paid close attention to currents and wind as we maneuvered through narrow passages. I looked at beautiful cloud formations building on the horizon and fretted they might signal a thunderstorm on the way.

If Duke ever doubted my abilities as commanding officer those first few weeks, he never showed it. He seemed at ease with my decisions, even though I sometimes privately was not. He let me do my job in my own way.

One afternoon while the yacht was anchored in a quiet cove, Duke entered the wheelhouse. He wanted to talk with his eldest son, Michael, back in Los Angeles over the radio telephone. I placed the call for him through the marine operator.

Michael was president of Batjac Productions, the film company Duke had set up to handle many of his later movies. The actor wanted to discuss some business with his son. I retreated to the wingdeck.

Unlike his younger brother Patrick, who'd served in the Coast Guard, Michael didn't have a great love of the sea. He didn't have much use for his father's yacht,

PAT STACY, DUKE'S SECRETARY AND GIRLFRIEND, CELEBRATES HER BIRTHDAY WITH DUKE IN THE GOOSE'S GALLEY AS KEN MIN-SHALL (FAR LEFT) AND CREWMAN LOOK ON. THE BOAT WAS IN SEATTLE, WASHINGTON, WHERE DUKE WAS FILMING McQ. *BERT MINSHALL PHOTO*

either. I believe he thought it was a cash drain on the Wayne resources.

A few minutes passed when I heard Duke raise his voice. It was the beginning of what sounded like an argument. Suddenly, in a very loud tone, Duke said angrily into the microphone, "Listen, Michael, the only asset you have at Batjac Productions is John Wayne!" I wondered what it was all about. Perhaps Duke wanted to remind his son just who buttered the company's bread.

By the time he signed off, though, it appeared that they'd resolved their differences. Business is business, I suppose, even between father and son. Duke put up the microphone in an amiable mood. He paused in the wheelhouse door as I signed off with the marine operator.

"Oh, Bert," he said, as I put up the receiver. I thought he was going to tell me of some chore that needed doing. "I just want to tell you that I think you're doing a helluva job."

He gave a wave of his hand, turned and headed aft, leaving a helluva pleased skipper behind.

•

By now Duke's secretary, Pat Stacy, had turned into something more than a person who simply took Duke's dictation and helped him with his mail and appointments. She was his girlfriend, for lack of a better word. Certainly she was company for Duke, someone who would help lessen the loneliness I know he felt after his separation from Pilar.

I haven't written too much about Pat in this book. This may seem odd considering that, from about 1973 on, she usually joined Duke on his cruises aboard the *Goose*. And yet, as pleasant as she was to be around, she just wasn't at the center of shipboard life. At least not for me. That was Duke's territory, and his children's.

There's been a lot written and a lot alleged about Pat's relationship to Duke. I wouldn't know about that. She traveled aboard ship with him, she shared his stateroom. Duke himself said he had "a very deep affection" for Pat. But was she really the last great love of his life, as she claims, or more of a ready companion, as do others? Perhaps the truth falls somewhere in between. I do know she was later the target of Duke's frustrations when he was sick and an outlet for his pain. She took it, and I suppose she genuinely loved him in spite of it.

All in all, as Duke might have said, she did pretty good in a tough spot. I think it best to leave it at that.

On the patio of Duke's Bayshore home. Left to right: secretary and close friend Pat Stacy, Newport Beach Porsche dealer Chick Iverson, Marisa, Duke and Ethan. *Bert Minshall photo*

•

We took the yacht back up north in the summer of 1978, but Duke never joined us. A lot had happened to him healthwise. Several months earlier doctors in Boston

had replaced a valve in his heart. They used a pig's valve, of all things, which made Duke joke that he could "oink with the best of them." He flew back home having cheated death once more, and when he stepped from his plane at Orange County Airport he was greeted by a tremendous throng of media and fans. His recovery went well, and he planned to fly up north and meet us for a few weeks' cruising. But then he came down with hepatitis and never made it.

The yacht was not idle in his absence, however. A charter was arranged with a group of realtors, and we took off for the inlets north of Vancouver. It was here several days later that we were unexpectedly boarded for inspection by a contingent of fish and game officers, as well as a group of Royal Canadian Mounted Police—unmounted for this occasion. At first I didn't even realize that these were the famous Mounties of popular legend. There wasn't a red tunic or flat-brimmed hat among them. Instead, they wore khaki shirts and pants, topped off with baseball-style caps. But as it turned out, they *were* about to get their man—or at least his liquor supply.

During the inspection tour it was discovered that the liquor locker in the forepeak was unsealed. (By law, visitors at the time could bring only one bottle of booze into Canada. For those coming in by yacht, the rest had to be sealed in a room or cabinet by customs officials.) As the officials looked upon the dozens of bottles of tequila, scotch and wine crammed into this compartment, it must have looked as if we were trying to sneak half a liquor store past them. They immediately impounded the yacht, ordering us to drop anchor until a fine of eight hundred dollars was paid.

I explained that the customs official in Victoria, during his inspection of the ship, decided not to seal the locker as a courtesy to Duke. But the Mounties were unsympathetic. They proceeded to confiscate about fifteen hundred dollars' worth of Duke's personal liquor. There was no reasoning with them. Finally, to get them off the yacht, I had to pay the eight-hundred-dollar fine out of my own funds and the ship's petty cash.

When I phoned Duke with news of the incident he was livid.

"Why, those bunch of jerks!" he exploded. It was the first time he'd ever had any problem with the Canadian authorities. Although he was resigned to paying the fine, he considered the confiscation of his booze a personal insult.

News of the yacht's "smuggling" scandal somehow leaked out. The papers in Los Angeles and Orange County all carried the story. Although it was quite embarrassing to me personally, I was more upset that any appearance of wrongdoing should attach itself to Duke.

On our return to Newport Beach I sent off a blistering letter to the Canadian authorities protesting the confiscation and the fine. Duke had reimbursed me the money I'd paid out, but I still felt we'd been shabbily treated.

Several weeks later I received a reply from the Canadian officials. In it they admitted they'd acted hastily and assured me they would reimburse Mr. Wayne for the full value of the liquor. However, they would not waive the fine.

When the reimbursement check finally arrived, it was several hundred dollars short—the customs office had calculated the refund without regard to the difference in exchange rates between Canadian and U.S. currencies.

Except for the run-in with our booze-nabbing Mounties, the trip to British Columbia had been wonderful. Princess Louisa Inlet was never more breathtaking. Duke said he wished he'd been able to make it up for a few weeks.

"Well, that's okay," he said, sitting on a sofa in his wood-paneled den. "We'll go next year."

It was a promise Duke would not keep. In the spring of 1979 he was admitted to UCLA Medical Center, dying of cancer. Even as he reassured me that afternoon he would be making another trip, he looked drawn and tired.

I didn't want to face it at the time, but my long journey with Duke aboard the *Wild Goose* was coming to an end.

DUKE ARRIVES AT ORANGE COUNTY AIRPORT AFTER UNDERGOING HEART SURGERY IN BOSTON IN 1978. THIS AIRPORT WOULD BE RENAMED JOHN WAYNE AIRPORT AFTER HIS DEATH. *UPI/BETTMANN*

The Long Voyage Home

Duke's last movie, *The Shootist*, was a film laced with irony and premonition for the actor. A legendary gunfighter—a shootist—is dying of cancer. But rather than waste away from his illness, he chooses to go out with guns blazing during a shootout with three other gunmen.

It must have been a difficult part emotionally for Duke to play. It hit too close to home. It reminded him of his own bout with the Big C twelve years earlier. As he later told a newspaper reporter, it touched a fear in him that the cancer would someday return.

When I saw The *Shootist* in a Newport Beach theater, I was moved by Duke's performance. It was haunting, sad, heroic. There was one scene that especially affected me.

It takes place at the breakfast table in widow Bond Rogers' boarding house. Mrs. Rogers—played by Lauren Bacall—is talking with Duke's character, gunfighter John Bernard Books, who has settled in one of her rooms to pass his last week of life on earth.

The widow, on edge, her emotions caught up in this strange man's lonely vigil, demands of him, "Who do you think you are?" It's really an unfinished question, though. It should be, "Who do you think you are . . . coming into my life, making me care for you, and now having this happen to you?" Books understands her hidden meaning and tells her the simple, unanswerable truth.

"I'm a dying man scared of the dark."

I don't know if that line echoed Duke's feelings as the dark fast approached him. As he told writer Wayne Warga while he was making *The Shootist*, "Sometimes the irony of this film gets to me."

Others have recorded in rather gruesome detail the progression of Duke's final illnesses. There was the heart surgery in 1978, hard followed by the discovery that he had stomach cancer. The surgeons removed his destroyed stomach, but they could not stop the spread of the disease.

As might be expected, that final year he used the *Wild Goose* less as his health deteriorated. He lacked the stamina for long cruises. Even short jaunts to Catalina proved taxing. He was spending too much time in hospitals.

Still, the big minesweeper had remained a sort of symbol to him, a symbol of the day when he'd be okay again and could once again cruise the Pacific coast he loved so much. He'd call me from time to time wanting to know the latest shipboard news. He always said that when he got better we'd go on a long trip. Probably up north.

"Damn, Bert," he told me once. "I want to beat this."

On April 10, 1979, Duke appeared on the Oscar telecast as a presenter. It would be his last public appearance.

The next day I talked with him on the patio of the Bayshore estate. He told me he wanted to use the yacht for a trip to Catalina that weekend. It was Easter. He thought a holiday cruise with the kids and a few close friends would be nice.

We watched the boats sailing past as we made light conversation. I told him I'd seen the Oscar show. I thought it had gone well.

"Yeah, it was okay," he agreed. He was shockingly thin. It had been three months since his stomach was removed. The surgeons had fashioned a new one using the top of his large intestine. He couldn't eat much. He said he had no real appetite. He couldn't drink liquor anymore. His appearance today upset me. However, I tried to act casual.

Duke was discussing the telecast.

"I was in trouble there for a moment," he said. "I almost tripped coming down all those stairs. I could hardly see where I was going the lighting was so bad." I suppose he meant that it had shined in his eyes, blinding him.

On the television show I recalled Duke striding down that long series of steps to the stage at the Dorothy Chandler Pavilion in Los Angeles, where the award presentation was held. He did it easily, smoothly. Now I shuddered to think that he might have taken a tumble at any moment. Few people watching that night could have realized just how closely he was courting disaster.

Talk turned to the *Wild Goose*. After his stomach operation he no longer talked about making that "long trip" up north he'd so looked forward to. Instead, he began to talk of selling the yacht. He hadn't made a movie in a long time. He thought it might be awhile before he made another. He said she was getting too expensive to keep and that he might have a buyer lined up soon.

"I've just got to get rid of that boat," he said. He explained how the IRS had made it nearly impossible to own a large yacht.

We were both silent for what seemed a long time.

"I hate to see her go," he finally said, looking out across the water toward Lido Isle. "I sure love that old boat. I wouldn't sell her unless I really had to."

I didn't know what to say. It seemed important that I let him know just how much he and the yacht meant to me. But how could I put sixteen years of my life into a few awkward sentences? I never felt so low as at that moment.

"I'm sorry to hear that, Duke," I managed, trying hard to control my emotions. "If I go with the boat when she sells, I'll miss working for you very much."

Duke looked at me and smiled.

"I'll miss having you around, Bert."

•

IT WAS A BEAUTIFUL SATURDAY MORNING THAT LAST WEEKEND OFF CATALINA. I WAS IN the wheelhouse listening to the radio when Duke emerged from his stateroom. Even as ill as he was, he still tried dutifully to get in a few laps around the boatdeck.

But right now he had something else on his mind. He climbed the three steps to the wingdeck and paused outside the wheelhouse door, looking in at me. As I joined him I saw he was holding a small cassette tape recorder.

"Listen," he said as he placed the recorder on the caprail and turned it on. I'd never seen it before. It looked brand new. I thought perhaps he was just showing it off. But to my dismay his recorded voice reeled off a list of complaints he'd taped during the night. They were just little irritations really, such as the steward's forgetting to leave some drinking water by his bed and a couple of small maintenance jobs aboard ship that needed attending to.

When the recitation of shipboard crimes was finished, he clicked off the machine. Then he picked it up and walked off.

I was quite upset until I realized that Duke at this time was in almost constant pain. In recent years, when his health rapidly started to fail, he'd grown noticeably more irritable. Little things could set him off. At times he could be almost cruel. This morning I just happened to be the most ready target. Last night he probably couldn't sleep and so turned to the recorder to pass the time.

Those of us close to Duke understood his grouchiness. He was on heavy medication all the time now. He admitted that it tended to make him short-tempered. He blamed the "witches' brew" of drugs his doctors had prescribed for him for his sometimes abrupt shifts of mood.

"It'd turn a Sunday school teacher into a sonofabitch," he once apologized.

On Easter Sunday Duke decided to go for a hike across the isthmus at Two Harbors. It was here so many years before that he'd raised hell with friends like Ward Bond, Vic McLaglen and Pappy Ford. Today he wore a white, V-neck sweater stitched with the logo from his John Wayne Tennis Club and a white golf cap. He'd lost so much weight his collar hung loose around his neck. He started across the half-mile-wide isthmus with Ethan and Marisa, but he was so weak he couldn't make it. He was forced to hitch a ride back in a car. I returned with him to the *Goose* in the British Dory. He was laughing and talking as if nothing were wrong. But he

immediately went to his stateroom to rest before dinner.

We left Catalina early the next morning. It had been a quiet weekend for Duke. He'd gone ashore in Avalon and the isthmus. He'd played gin rummy and backgammon. He'd talked with friends on the afterdeck, reminiscing about other places and other times. He'd done nothing strenuous. But when we pulled into the slip back at Lido Anchorage he looked all done in. He was bone tired.

I saw him off at the boarding steps.

"Thanks, Bert," he said. "I had a nice time."

Then he walked slowly up the dock to his waiting station wagon. It was the last time I ever saw him.

•

When Duke was in Hoag Hospital in Newport Beach just before his last trip to the UCLA Medical Center, I went to visit him. I took with me a large, beautiful picture book of the Los Hados Hotel in Manzanillo, Mexico. It had been given to me by the manager of the hotel, who was visiting in the States for a few days. The hotel was a favorite stopping place of Duke's. The manager wanted me to give it to him. I said I would.

At the hospital reception desk I was told Duke was sleeping. Apparently the last few days had been rough. I thought about waiting, but I hated the idea of bothering him now. So I left the book at the reception desk with instructions to give it to him when he was feeling better. Then I left.

As it turned out I should have waited. At UCLA his condition went from bad to worse. I hated hospitals. I kept making excuses about waiting to visit him until he improved. At the same time, I'd heard from others that Michael Wayne was restricting visitors. This was probably necessary to a certain extent to help Duke conserve his energy. Yet some of his oldest friends, such as Joe DeFranco, who had spent many happy days cruising with Duke aboard the *Goose*, reportedly were shut out. I heard that even Mary St. John had to sneak in to see him. If that was the case, my chances of getting a few minutes with Duke didn't look good.

Duke aboard the *Searcher*
somewhere off Mexico.

Perhaps I could have used Marisa or Ethan in an attempt to run the blockade, but I didn't want to be the cause of any more tension for the family. They had enough to cope with as it was. And, selfishly, I suppose, I really didn't think I could take seeing Duke lying in a hospital bed with all those tubes running out of him, helpless, wasting away. Right or wrong, I never made that trip to Los Angeles. I never got to tell Duke good-bye.

But then, I'm not sure that's what Duke would have wanted to hear from me, anyway.

•

JACK HEADLEY ONCE TOLD ME ABOUT AN EPIC BATTLE DUKE PUT UP TRYING TO LAND a marlin off Mexico. Jack was engineer at the time of the ninety-five-foot *Searcher*, owned by a friend of Duke's. It wasn't too long after the actor's lung-cancer operation in 1964.

According to Jack, Duke was trolling about mid-morning when his line was hit hard by a huge marlin. The actor shouted with excitement as he started to work the big fish. Jack knew he had a struggle ahead of him landing it, but no one aboard could have predicted the tremendous fight that followed.

Duke would reel in, pumping the pole with all his might, gaining line steadily when suddenly the fish would make a lightning run back out to sea, taking line with it in a whirl from off the reel. The seesaw battle went on for hours. Sweat soaked Duke's shirt. He was gasping for breath. Everyone on board could see that this powerful fish was getting the better of him. His one lung put him at a great disadvantage. But he wouldn't give up.

The exhausting battle dragged on. There was a quiet, serious discussion among the others about what to do. Finally, it was decided that the skipper would maneuver the boat so Duke's line would pass underneath and be cut by the props. The skipper would try to make it look like an accident, but he knew he'd catch holy hell from Duke just the same.

Then, as the skipper revved the engines, Duke's line, after so much unrelieved strain, suddenly went slack. The marlin had slipped free. Duke's gut-wrenching struggle was over. He'd failed to boat his fish, but he was too tired to care. He'd been going on sheer guts at the end.

Jack said Duke was so exhausted that he went to his cabin and didn't reappear until well into the next day.

"But Duke would've died rather than give up the fight," he said, shaking his head in amazement. "He just wouldn't quit."

On June 11, 1979, at the UCLA Medical Center, John Wayne died of complications from cancer.

•

ABOUT MIDNIGHT THE PHONE RANG. IT WAS AISSA. "HELLO, BERT. I'M OVER AT MOM'S." Her voice sounded small and far away. There was a pause. "We just got back from the hospital. Ethan and Marisa are here with us. Would you like to come over?"

Five minutes later I was on my way to Pilar's home in Big Canyon. I was still numb. I'd heard the news earlier on the television, how it was all over. I wondered if Ken had heard. I doubted it. He was somewhere off Alaska in his fishing boat.

I suppose it shouldn't have come as a shock, but somehow I'd always expected Duke to make it through okay. He'd always done it before. I knew things looked very bad. Yet that stubborn hope that he'd recover had never really left me. I was watching one of the network tributes to the actor, alone with my thoughts, when Aissa called.

The guard at the private gate to Big Canyon checked my name on a list and motioned me through. I drove along the winding streets to Pilar's home.

Pilar met me at the front door. We hugged each other in the hallway, and finally, my English reserve all but gone, I broke down and cried in her arms. Pilar told me it was okay, that it was for the best, that Duke was no longer in pain. After a few minutes I regained my composure. I went into the den where the children were waiting.

As I hugged them they seemed like my own kids. We'd spent so much time together. I loved them all very much.

We sat on the sofas by the unlit fireplace and recalled the good times we'd shared aboard the *Wild Goose*. Someone mentioned the colored eggs that Duke used to like to hide around the ship on Easter morning for the kids to find. He had taken as much delight in the hunt as his children had. There were a lot of memories. Once or twice Aissa started to cry softly.

It was after five a.m. when I finally stood up to leave. Poor little Marisa, exhausted by emotion and the late hour, had been put to bed a couple of hours earlier. Ethan and Aissa looked as if they were ready to follow. Pilar saw me to the door.

"Thank you for coming over, Bert," she said. She took my hand a moment before leaving me on the front porch.

As I walked to my car I saw the sky was starting to lighten. The sun would be up soon. I thought of the *Wild Goose* at her mooring not more than fifteen minutes away. Duke had always liked early mornings aboard the yacht. He once told me it was his favorite time of day. I started the engine and backed out of the driveway.

Then I drove home through the empty streets of Newport.

John Wayne and the Wild Goose 163

Epilogue

Duke lies in an unmarked grave on a hillside overlooking Newport Beach. At the time of the funeral, the papers reported that the family feared grave robbers. So the plot at Pacific View Memorial Park was left purposely bare of any identifying headstone or monument. It remains so to this day.

The funeral itself was attended by only close relatives and a few friends. There are those—including Pilar—who said Duke always wanted to be cremated and his ashes strewn in the ocean between Newport and Catalina. And that instead of a funeral, he wanted his friends and loved ones to hold a big happy Irish wake with plenty of food and booze and jokes to remember him by. If that's so, he didn't get what he wanted. Michael Wayne was in charge of the arrangements.

Regardless, Duke ended up in pretty good company at Pacific View, for Pete Stein lies just down the hill, as does little Billy Sweatt, who died in 1981. On Billy's headstone is engraved a silhouette of a large yacht—clearly the *Wild Goose*. Duke would have liked that. Chick Iverson, Jr., is here, too, his grave—in the words of Aissa Wayne—acting as a signpost to Duke's. I suppose one day I'll end up at Pacific View with Duke and my shipmates—although, to paraphrase ornery Rooster Cogburn at the end of *True Grit*, I hope no one will mind if I take my time about doing so.

On the fourth anniversary of Duke's death, I went to visit his grave. It was a gray, somewhat chilly June afternoon. Almost Liverpool weather, I thought, pulling into the parking lot. It was after the cemetery's closing time, but I hopped a chain strung across the road leading up to the gravesites.

Climbing the hillside where I knew the grave to be, I circled for a few minutes before finding Chick Jr.'s headstone. A moment later I was standing over Duke's plot. I had no flowers with me. I just wanted to be there and think for a little while.

The grass covering the grave had filled in and blended with the surrounding growth. It was hard to think of Duke beneath those thick green blades. It seemed like an awful small place to hold such a big man. I looked out toward the harbor. Beyond, the low June clouds seemed to merge with the ocean. I turned and walked back down the hill.

As I passed the flagpole at the cemetery's entrance I saw a small pot of red flowers at its base with a card attached. I walked over and read the careful handwriting on it. There were just two lines.

> JOHN WAYNE—
> LEST WE FORGET

It was unsigned. It was a moment before I recognized that phrase. It was from one

of Duke's finest films, *She Wore A Yellow Ribbon*. In the John Ford-directed picture, Duke's character, Captain Nathan Brittles, is about to retire after a long career in the U.S. cavalry. Before he leaves his fort for a new life in California, however, his men present him with a silver watch, inscribed, "To Capt. Brittles from C Company—Lest we forget." It's a particularly moving scene, played with deep feeling by Duke.

I looked back up the hillside toward Duke's grave. I don't know why, but my mind went back a dozen years to a lovely summer morning during one of the *Goose's* northern trips. The big yacht was sailing along a mirror-like inlet. I was in the wheelhouse with Duke when he impulsively asked the skipper, Jack Headley, to open up the throttle.

"C'mon, Skipper," he laughed. "Let's see what the old girl will do."

Duke then turned to me and suggested I take the Whaler and get the speed trial on film, just in case "we blow 'er up." I raced off to grab my 8-mm movie camera.

A few minutes later, as a deckhand drove the Whaler, I steadied myself in the bow with my camera. We were holding just off the yacht's starboard side when I saw a great cloud of black smoke billow from the stack. Jack was pouring the coals to her. As the *Goose* edged up to flank speed and the carbon burned from the engines, the smoke changed to bluish-white. The big yacht must have been doing fourteen or fifteen knots. I doubt if she'd ever moved so fast. A spray of water arched up and out from the racing bow.

The navy workhorse looked magnificent against the beautiful backdrop of inlet and forest. Just then a figure walked out onto the wheelhouse wingdeck. It was Duke. He stood there a moment, a great smile on his face, still vibrant, still a long way from death, delighted as his beloved *Wild Goose* barreled through the still water.

"Lest We Forget," read the card with the flowers at the cemetery's entrance.

Bloody small chance of that.

Postscript

It is local legend that the ghost of John Wayne stalks the decks of the *Wild Goose* even now, a supernatural presence of a man who was bigger than life while he was alive, on a ship he loved beyond all others. The week before Wayne died, the *Wild Goose* was sold to a Santa Monica lawyer and the story of the ghostly presence was heard soon after. In December 1979, the new owner moved the yacht to San Pedro and later to a mooring buoy in Long Beach Harbor, where it stayed until 1991.

That year a Newport Beach resident, Deil Gustafson, bought the vessel and has undertaken major repair and began renovation efforts to overcome a dozen more years of aging since John Wayne sold it and to make it both seaworthy and aesthetically pleasing after almost fifty years of

use. But the spirit of John Wayne and his affection for the ship were respected even as interior renovations were made, with numerous shipboard features of Wayne's ownership preserved and his memory enhanced with paintings and other memorabilia. If his ghost does not really walk the decks, his aura is, nevertheless, present. The yacht currently is docked in Marina Del Rey and, as in Wayne's day, is available for charter.

On June 20, 1979, Orange County Airport was renamed "John Wayne Airport, Orange County" by the county board of supervisors. In 1982 a $300,000, nine-foot-tall bronze statue of John Wayne was installed at the airport in an outdoor ceremony attended by all seven of the Wayne children, as well as by Pilar Wayne and Captain Bert Minshall. The statue, depicting a striding John Wayne dressed in Western garb, has since been moved to a

prominent location in the airport's new terminal building.

Captain Bert Minshall remained as the *Wild Goose*'s skipper for a year before leaving to assume command of another 136-foot converted minesweeper, *Nesco I*, which was berthed next to the *Wild Goose* in Newport Beach for many years. In 1984 he became captain of the fifty-four-foot *Touchdown*, the personal yacht of Georgia Frontiere, owner of the Los Angeles Rams' football team. Since 1989 he has been skipper of the seventy-foot *Mariah*, based in Marina Del Rey and owned by film director Blake Edwards (*The Pink Panther*, *10*, *Victor/Victoria*) and his wife, singer-actress Julie Andrews.

Aissa Wayne lives in Newport Beach, as does her mother, Pilar. Marisa Wayne is married and lives in Colorado. Ethan Wayne lives in Newport Beach and is pursuing an acting career.

ABOVE: ALTHOUGH NO PHOTOS ARE KNOWN TO EXIST OF THE *WILD GOOSE* AS A NAVY MINESWEEPER, HER SISTER SHIP THE *NESCO I* (PICTURED) SHARED THE SAME HULL AND DESIGN. *U.S. NAVY PHOTO*

LEFT: *THE GOOSE*—THEN KNOWN AS *LA BEVERIE*—SHORTLY AFTER HER CONVERSION INTO A PRIVATE YACHT IN THE LATE 1940s.

UPPER LEFT: THE YACHT AS SHE APPEARS TODAY.

OPPOSITE: DOCKED AT HER NEW HOME IN MARINA DEL REY, CALIFORNIA.

Naval Background and Technical Features
of the *Wild Goose* to 1979

CONSTRUCTION
Shipyard: Ballard Marine Railway Company
Location: Seattle, Washington
Keel laid: July 6, 1942
Launched: December 19, 1942
Completed: May 26, 1943

NAVAL BACKGROUND
Classification: Motor Minesweeper YMS 328,
    U.S. Navy (there were 481 total vessels in
    this class)
Operations area: Aleutian Islands, Alaska
Guns: (1) 3-inch 50-mm bow; (2) 20-mm
Complement: 4 officers; 29 enlisted men
Retirement: Struck from Naval Vessel Register
    October 29, 1946 (sent to mothball fleet)
Sold: January 16, 1948, to Hal Jones of Seattle,
    who undertook first conversion to private
    yacht; second owner, Max Wyman; third
    owner, John Wayne

HULL
Composition: 3" Douglas fir
Overall length: 136 feet
Beam: 25 feet
Draft: 9 feet
Displacement: 287 tons
Rudders: 2

ENGINES
2 G.M.C. Cleveland 8-268-A straight eight
    cylinder diesels
Total shaft horsepower: 1,000 (500-hp each)

SPEED
11 knots cruising; 13 knots maximum cruising
    (attainable flank speed: 14–15 knots)
FUEL
10,000 gallons. Range: 3,500 miles

FRESH WATER
3,000 gallons in two tanks
Added capacity: 40 gallons an hour from two
    watermakers
Two shipboard fresh-water-pressure systems

COMMUNICATIONS AND NAVIGATION
Apelco transmitter and receiver
RCA 10-channel transceiver Teletype
    Loran "C"
Raytheon indicating and recording fathometer
Raytheon 48-mile radar Weatherfax equipment

OTHER EQUIPMENT
Complete shipboard machine shop
Walk-in freezer
4 generators
16-foot Boston Whaler, 115-hp; 17-foot British
    Dory, 135-hp

ACCOMMODATIONS
Upper deck: 1 master stateroom with attached
    2-bunk cabin
Main deck: 1 single, 1 double
Lower deck: 1 triple, 1 double
    Captain's cabin
    First mate's cabin
    Crew: 4 bunks
Total accommodations: 12 guest; 6 crew